THE POLITICS OF FAITH AND
THE POLITICS OF SCEPTICISM

Selected Writings of Michael Oakeshott

General editor:

Timothy Fuller

Also available:

The Voice of Liberal Learning: Michael Oakeshott on Education
(introduced and edited by Timothy Fuller)

Morality and Politics in Modern Europe: The Harvard Lectures
(edited by Shirley Robin Letwin)

Religion, Politics and the Moral Life
(introduced and edited by Timothy Fuller)

THE POLITICS OF FAITH
AND THE
POLITICS OF SCEPTICISM

Michael Oakeshott

Edited by Timothy Fuller

YALE UNIVERSITY PRESS
NEW HAVEN AND LONDON 1996

Set in Linotron Baskerville by Best-set Typesetter Ltd, Hong Kong
Printed and bound in Great Britain by The Bath Press, Avon

Library of Congress Cataloging-in-Publication Data

Oakeshott, Michael Joseph, 1901–1990
    The politics of faith and the politics of scepticism/Michael
Oakeshott; edited by Timothy Fuller.
    Includes bibliographical references and index.
    ISBN 0–300–06625–2 (alk. paper)
    1. Political science—Philosophy.   2. Political science.
I. Fuller, Timothy, 1940– .   II. Title.   III. Series: Oakeshott,
Michael Joseph, 1901– Selections.   1993.
JA71.O23   1996
320'.01—dc20   96–3852
                                                        CIP

A catalogue record for this book is available from the British Library.

CONTENTS

ACKNOWLEDGEMENTS

I want to acknowledge Professors Owen Cramer, Robert McJimsey, Carol Neel and Elmer Peterson of Colorado College and Professor Stuart Warner of Roosevelt University for advice as I prepared this work for publication. They bear no responsibility for the results. I also express special appreciation to Marianna McJimsey for once again providing a fine index.

Timothy Fuller

EDITOR'S INTRODUCTION

Political philosophy cannot be expected to increase our ability to be successful in political activity. It will not help us to distinguish between good and bad political projects; it has no power to guide or to direct us in the enterprise of pursuing the intimations of our tradition. But the patient analysis of the general ideas which have come to be connected with political activity – ideas such as nature, artifice, reason, will, law, authority, obligation, etc. – in so far as it succeeds in removing some of the crookedness from our thinking and leads to a more economical use of concepts, is an activity neither to be overrated nor despised. But it must be understood as an explanatory, not a practical, activity, and if we pursue it, we may only hope to be less often cheated by ambiguous statement and irrelevant argument.
                                    – from 'Political Education' (1951)

The Politics of Faith and the Politics of Scepticism presents the reader with a strikingly fresh and unexpected expression of Michael Oakeshott's thought on modern politics and government. It is the book of which his 1951 Inaugural Lecture at the London School of Economics, 'Political Education', is a kind of summary. His explicit design is to consider what governing and being governed have meant in modern European politics. He puts aside the question 'Who shall rule and by what authority?' in favour of understanding how we have answered the question 'What shall government do?'[1]

---

[1] (p. 3) 'The modern history of European politics', Oakeshott remarks, 'has most frequently been composed with attention fixed on the first of these questions . . . And this story has been told so often and so eloquently that we are near to being persuaded that it is the whole story . . . But . . . there is no simple and direct relation to be discerned between the constitution and pursuits of government' (p. 3).

Michael Oakeshott died in December 1990. In May 1991, Shirley Letwin and I went to his cottage on the Dorset coast to retrieve the papers he had left her, in his will, to do with as she thought best. We found a much greater number of papers than we had expected – including the typescript of this work – and brought back about half of all that we found to Shirley Letwin's house in London. A few weeks later I returned to the cottage with Dr Robert Orr of the London School of Economics to retrieve the papers that remained. At Shirley Letwin's death, ownership of the papers passed to Professor William Letwin.

The work before us was typed on plain eight- by ten-inch paper. It has no title-page, but the choice of title is straightforward, given the subject and organization of the work. The division into chapters and the chapter titles are exactly as in the typescript. Typescript page thirty-six in chapter 5 is missing and we have not found it anywhere among the papers.

The script, 232 pages in length, is not continuously paginated. The 'Introduction', and the first two chapters are continuously numbered 1 to 118. The next two chapters and the conclusion are separately numbered: 1 to 39, 1 to 47, 1 to 30. The work as we have it is a continuous whole, however, typed on a single kind of paper apparently on a single typewriter. With some of Oakeshott's works we have a handwritten version of a manuscript that was later typed, but have not found such a version in this case. What we have is undated, but its central theme Oakeshott already expressed in the 1930s. In *The Social and Political Doctrines of Contemporary Europe*, he writes:

> With regard to the moral ideals represented in these doctrines, the fundamental cleavage appears to me to lie neither between those which offer a spiritual ideal and those which offer a material ideal, nor in the actual content of the moral ideals themselves, but between those which hand over to the arbitrary will of a society's self-appointed leaders the planning of its entire life, and those which not only refuse to hand over the destiny of society to any set of officials but also consider the whole notion of planning the destiny of a society to be both stupid and immoral. On the one side are the three modern authoritarian doctrines, Communism, Fascism, and National Socialism; on the other Catholicism and Liberalism. To the Liberal and the Catholic mind alike the notion that men can authoritatively plan and impose a way of life upon a society appears to be a piece of pretentious ignorance; it can be entertained only by men who

have no respect for human beings and are willing to make them the means to the realization of their own ambitions.[2]

The work was elaborated after World War II and completed probably in 1952. The themes developed here correspond frequently to those of the essays Oakeshott wrote between 1947 and 1951, and which he brought together in *Rationalism in Politics* in 1962. He refers to the Education Act of 1944 and to Huizinga's *Homo Ludens*, which he could have read in German in the 1940s, and very likely read in the English translation published in England in 1949. His footnotes are characteristically barebones, and most of them appear here without amendments, as they appeared in the original. One mistaken reference (footnotes 8 and 9 on pp. 103 and 104) to the *Cambridge Economic History of Europe* (first published in 1941) turns out actually to be a reference to a book by Lionel Robbins, *The Theory of Economic Policy in English Classical Political Economy* of 1952. I am indebted to Professor Stuart Warner for helping me to track down the actual source of Oakeshott's reference to Robbins's work.

Among my acquaintances who knew Oakeshott far longer than I, there is no one, including Shirley Letwin, who was aware of this script. It does not appear to have been presented as a lecture course. Oakeshott's papers include several courses of lectures, labelled by him as such. Two knowledgeable students of his work, who reviewed this script for the Yale University Press, were struck by its unexpectedness.

Why Oakeshott chose to leave this (and many other writings) unpublished – a question those interested in his work often discuss – is a mystery. Here is a finished exposition of his thinking at a certain stage. He may have been displeased with it in some way. He was often dissatisfied with or uncertain about his writing, and revised the essays he did publish numerous times, often over many years, before letting them see the light of day. However, he put no restrictions on what was to be done with his papers when he bequeathed them to Shirley Letwin. *The Voice of Liberal Learning* was published with his full consultation and approval in 1989, and although he died shortly before the new, expanded edition of *Rationalism in Politics* was published in 1991, he had seen it in preparation and had approved its additions and

---

[2] Michael Oakeshott, *The Social and Political Doctrines of Contemporary Europe* (Cambridge: Cambridge University Press, 1939), footnote 1, pp. xxii–xxiii.

reorganization. He was pleased with these projects, but he would not have undertaken them himself.

Oakeshott was ambitious to write essays of lasting import in political philosophy, and he thought he had. In his portrait in Gonville and Caius College, Cambridge, he sits at a table on which *On Human Conduct* is prominently and centrally displayed. Yet he did not show ambition in the ways that are typical of academics. He did not much care for professional meetings; he had no urge – as is now abundantly evident – to publish everything he wrote.

This book, although neither an historical monograph nor a strictly philosophical essay, includes elements of both, and more. It is as close to a book of advice for the practice of modern politics as Oakeshott ever produced. Typically, it offers a way of thinking about politics without offering specific policies. But Oakeshott is at his most Aristotelian in suggesting that there is a manner of political conduct appropriate to striking a mean between extremes he identifies here as the 'politics of faith' and the 'politics of scepticism'. Like Aristotle, Oakeshott does not mean simply compromising differences; he means determining the proper balance between competing tendencies. In the modern context to him this meant reestablishing a balance against the dominant 'politics of faith', by revitalizing or bringing back to sight the virtues of the 'politics of scepticism'.

Oakeshott's approach is dialectical. He argues that, out of the array of efforts to explain to themselves what they were doing politically, Europeans produced two competing tendencies of thought about government's purpose while using a political vocabulary which, because common to both, is ambiguous.[3] The practical meaning of political terms thus came to depend, and still depends, on how we mediate the two opposing ways of thinking about the purposes and scope of government which emerged in opposition to each other in early modern European history. The politics of faith, Oakeshott goes on to assert, has dominated political thought and action for the past 150 years, putting the politics of scepticism on the defensive. This, he thought, could end only in the disappointment of self-defeat for the practitioners of the politics of faith.

---

[3] 'Democracy', for example, suggests both the means to limit political power, and a plebiscitary device to legitimate the concentrated, extensive use of power.

The 'faith' in question is virtually the opposite of traditional religious faith. It is faith in the capacity of human beings to perfect themselves through their own efforts, made possible by the discovery of ways continually to increase the power of government as the essential instrumentality to control, design and perfect individuals and groups. 'The prime condition', Oakeshott tells us, 'of the emergence of the politics of faith', was 'a remarkable and intoxicating increase of human power' making its appearance at the beginning of modern history, which stimulated the hope of salvation through politics, and the Baconian promise of prosperity, abundance and welfare. This 'faith' would supplant the Augustinian understanding of faith which opposes Pelagianism and worldliness. The politics of faith corresponds, in short, to that modern disposition Oakeshott otherwise called 'rationalism in politics' or the 'ideological style of politics'.[4]

The 'scepticism' in question finds human experience to be so varied and complex that no plan for ordering and reconstructing human affairs could ever succeed. Such plans at best yield temporary exhilaration and evanescent accomplishments, and at their worst oppress subjects and depress the human spirit. The range of human experience, and the interminable altering of relations among individuals and groups, will always outstrip every effort to bring them under the control of a central design. To increase governmental power is to stimulate the mistaken aspiration to expand such control in order, collectively, to 'pursue perfection as the crow flies'.[5] This threatens the distinctive modern engagement of individual human beings to gain self-understanding for themselves, and to explore the immense opportunities opened up for individuals who insist on responding to the world according to what it means to them, individuals who see themselves as free because they know they are 'in themselves what they are for themselves'.[6] Under the latter

---

[4] In 'Political Education', and in the title essay of Michael Oakeshott, *Rationalism in Politics* (New York: Basic Books, 1962; new and expanded edn, Indianapolis: Liberty Press, 1991).

[5] See 'The Tower of Babel', in *Rationalism in Politics*.

[6] 'A Place of Learning' (1974), in Michael Oakeshott, *The Voice of Liberal Learning: Michael Oakeshott on Education*, ed. Timothy Fuller (New Haven and London: Yale University Press), 1989, p. 19, and also 'The Claims of Politics', 1939, in Michael Oakeshott, *Religion, Politics and the Moral Life*, ed. Timothy Fuller (New Haven and London: Yale University Press, 1993).

conditions, Oakeshott sympathized with individuals who pursue their own perfection as the crow flies. A world of individuals may compose many melodies, but they cannot be orchestrated by a single composer or team of composers, even ones of genius.

All this emerges in the course of an extended reflection, informed by historical and philosophic study, on the peculiarities of the practices, the talk, and the considered writings that have constituted political activity, and reflection on political activity, in Europe, and especially Britain, since the fifteenth century. While Oakeshott acknowledged that the features of modern European politics have spread across the world in the twentieth century (universalizing the local ambivalence of conduct and ambiguity of political talk), he thought we could discern them most clearly in the European original.

We have, then, an exposition of the theme central to all of Oakeshott's post-World War II thought: the effort to theorize the animating if divided purposes of modern European politics and the modern European state. He developed this theme in other ways in his Harvard Lectures of 1958, published in 1993 as *Morality and Politics in Modern Europe,* and presented what he took to be his definitive statement in 1975 in *On Human Conduct.*[7]

The Politics of Faith and the Politics of Scepticism is related to the latter two works in seeking a comprehensive characterization of the terrain of modern politics. It resembles *On Human Conduct* in setting out two opposed ways of conceiving the scope of the activities of government. *On Human Conduct* analysed a basic opposition reflecting differences between two poles of thinking on the purpose of government. The modern state, Oakeshott thought, could best be understood through elaborating the competing ideal types of 'civil association' and 'enterprise association'. Each of these offered a different model of what governments are for and what they could be expected to accomplish.

---

[7] Michael Oakeshott, *Morality and Politics in Modern Europe,* ed. Shirley Robin Letwin (New Haven and London: Yale University Press), 1993. *On Human Conduct* (Oxford: The Clarendon Press), 1975. See also 'The Vocabulary of a Modern European State', in *Political Studies,* 1975. There was a second theme in the 1950s: to constrain the universalizing claims of modern rationalism by evoking the poetic sense of delight and contemplation. This came to fruition in *The Voice of Poetry in the Conversation of Mankind* (London: Bowes & Bowes), 1959.

The description of 'civil association' in *On Human Conduct* shows that it is compatible with a sceptical disposition in politics, and is a coherent model of how to respond to the modern political situation. People of divergent purposes who, nevertheless, must live together in the same polity, benefit from association based on civility and procedure rather than on a uniting purpose to which only some will ever willingly grant approval. Civility and procedure mitigate the dilemma of establishing proper distances among themselves.[8] Oakeshott thought 'enterprise association' an inappropriate model for the modern state since it presupposes a single, unifying purpose. Enterprise associations are proper for voluntary associations of individuals who subscribe to, and may also exit from, a common undertaking.

Morality and Politics in Modern Europe sought to undermine one of the main rationales for increasing the power of governments by showing that people who have come to see themselves as individuals cannot perfect themselves through imposing a communitarian addition on an individualist base. This is because the self-understanding required for individuality cannot be reconciled with the implications of the wish for communality. When the synthesis is attempted, a bastardized pseudo-order results. There is no recovering what some moderns imagined to be an accessible classical or medieval alternative. Oakeshott showed why an amalgamation of these alternatives will never be satisfactory.

In *The Politics of Faith and the Politics of Scepticism* he appraises

---

[8] Oakeshott gave succinct expression to this: 'There was once, so Schopenhauer tells us, a colony of porcupines. They were wont to huddle together on a cold winter's day and, thus wrapped in communal warmth, escape being frozen. But, plagued with the pricks of each other's quills, they drew apart. And every time the desire for warmth brought them together again, the same calamity overtook them. Thus they remained, distracted between two misfortunes, able neither to tolerate nor to do without one another, until they discovered that when they stood at a certain distance from one another they could both delight in one another's individuality and enjoy one another's company. They did not attribute any metaphysical significance to this distance, nor did they imagine it to be an independent source of happiness, like finding a friend. They recognized it to be a relationship in terms not of substantive enjoyments but of contingent considerations that they must determine for themselves. Unknown to themselves, they had invented civil association.' 'Talking Politics' (1975), in *Rationalism in Politics* (1991 edn), pp. 460–61.

the historical basis of these sorts of antipathy. Oakeshott's view on the conflict between individualist and communal sentiments resembles Benjamin Constant's distinction in 'The Liberty of the Ancients Compared with That of the Moderns', an essay he admired.[9]

At the same time, *The Politics of Faith and the Politics of Scepticism* constitutes a significant attempt to organize into a single expression the diverse arguments of Oakeshott's well-known essays of the 1940s and 1950s.[10] Convinced as he was of the advantages of the essay style, especially as practised by Montaigne, Oakeshott chose in that period to publish occasional essays, guarding against what, to him if not to others, might have appeared to be a too systematic exposition of his thought. In the period of his intense criticism of 'rationalism' from the end of World War II down to the publication of *Rationalism in Politics* in 1962, he consciously did not accede to the prevailing academic style. He wanted to avoid rationalist criticism of rationalism.[11] Nevertheless, he continued through that period to write also in a more systematic fashion, as is now evident. *The Politics of Faith and the Politics of Scepticism* offers the alternative of a sustained expression. It complements the already published works, illuminating Oakeshott's thinking about modern politics and government, and adapting his view of the explanatory task of the philosophical student of politics as he had elaborated it in two essays of the 1940s, 'The Concept of a Philosophy of Politics' and 'Political Philosophy'.[12]

The polarity in manners of political thinking and conduct Oakeshott identified has not been resolved or superseded. Oakeshott thought this could only happen if one of these approaches to politics and government should find a way to end debate by vanquishing the other, thus freeing itself to move

---

[9] This essay or speech of 1819 can be found in Benjamin Constant, *Political Writings*, trans. and ed. Biancamaria Fontana (Cambridge: Cambridge University Press, 1988), pp. 308–28. In contrast, Rousseau's earlier effort to reconcile the conflict Oakeshott thought a failure.

[10] Readers of *Rationalism in Politics* will easily pick out themes and expressions from those essays throughout this book.

[11] He remarks of F. A. Hayek's *Road to Serfdom* that resistance to rationalism has there been 'converted to an ideology', and that 'a plan to resist all planning may be better than its opposite, but it belongs to the same style of politics'. *Rationalism in Politics* (New York: Basic Books), 1962 edn, p. 21; 1991 edn, p. 26.

[12] In Michael Oakeshott *Religion, Politics and the Moral Life*.

toward an extreme realization of its own aspiration. The opposition has been mediated in practice, however, in grudging acknowledgement of each other's presence, and fear of the extremes whenever they actually seem to threaten. Out of this was constituted the field on which political struggles are played out. Even in analysing the character of these alternatives, philosophically and historically, Oakeshott's intent was to show the basis for maintaining an equilibrium, or as he famously put it 'an even keel' for a ship set sail on a boundless and bottomless sea.[13] Indeed, this is the extended explanation of the arguments of his Inaugural Lecture of 1951. To keep an even keel, the value of the politics of scepticism must be restored to sight to inhibit the perils of excessive domination by the politics of faith. To choose the politics of scepticism is, then, not to engage in reactionary politics, but in a 'trimming act' of statesmanship. What practising politicians need is not a doctrine, but a view of the limits and possibilities of their situation.

Oakeshott did not think that exploring politics philosophically could produce a simple, unified doctrine. The philosophical study of politics, as he understood it, is not a higher, more abstract way to advocate policies. To attempt to understand politics philosophically is a fundamentally different engagement from attempting, by transposing the discussion of policy into theoretical terms, to justify specific actions. To understand politics philosophically is to understand from a perspective political actors cannot easily adopt. For the philosophic inquirer, whether drawn to one side or the other, can only present that inclination by disclosing the reasons he finds persuasive, exposing his position to further philosophic investigation. To seek more is to abandon philosophic reflection, preferring persuasion and action in place of an invitation to prolong an unfinished conversation. One cannot simply unify philosophical understanding with practical action. The attempt to do so will necessarily sacrifice the philosophic endeavour to understand:

---

[13] 'In political activity, then, men sail a boundless and bottomless sea; there is neither harbour for shelter nor floor for anchorage, neither starting-place nor appointed destination. The enterprise is to keep afloat on an even keel; the sea is both friend and enemy; and the seamanship consists in using the resources of a traditional manner of behaviour in order to make a friend of every hostile occasion.' *Rationalism in Politics*, 1962 edn, p. 127; 1991 edn, p. 60. He goes on to remark that this will seem 'unduly sceptical' to those with a plan or vision for the future.

the philosopher as philosopher can only pursue understanding for its own sake.[14]

Oakeshott's detachment lies in his explaining how each of the two ways of thinking achieves coherence based on assumptions it does not question. Inevitably, the operative assumptions of each way of thinking exclude other possible assumptions which, if included, would introduce explicit incoherence into one's practical understanding, constraining one's readiness to act, and opening to question the adequacy of one's knowledge of what to do.

His detachment is qualified, however, in his praise of Halifax's *The Character of a Trimmer*, which presents the one who has the knack of keeping the ship of state on an even keel. What Oakeshott found here was not absolute sceptical doubt but that moderation of expectations which marks practical as opposed to philosophical scepticism. The 'trimmer's' scepticism, confronted with the politics of faith, seeks to moderate conflict, for the need for change can be admitted without the stimulus of illusory expectations. 'The "trimmer" is one who disposes his weight so as to keep the ship upon an even keel . . . Being concerned to prevent politics from running to extremes . . . He will be found facing in whatever direction the occasion seems to require if the boat is to go even.'[15]

In using the terms 'politics of faith' and the 'politics of scepticism', Oakeshott sets aside the oft invoked dichotomy of 'ancients' and 'moderns';[16] the polar alternatives are, for him,

---

[14] Consider Oakeshott's analysis, in the early pages of *On Human Conduct*, of Plato's Allegory of the Cave. Oakeshott accepted the possibility of 'ascent' from the cave (but not the claim of a superior engagement), but he did not think the 'descent' brings back wisdom about how to reorganize the cave. For him, philosophy taught the flimsiness of human knowledge. He was a Socratic in this sense.

[15] (p. 123) Halifax's *The Character of a Trimmer* 'was one of many attempts to elicit the principle of "moderation" from the conditions of modern politics . . . For although the sceptical style is itself an extreme, its extremity is not to impose a single pattern of activity upon a community, and consequently it enjoys . . . a characteristic forbearance of its own which can be seen to intimate a wider doctrine of moderation' (pp. 122–3).

[16] 'I shall be concerned only with modern politics. Some features of modern politics no doubt have their counterpart elsewhere; in the ancient world, for example. But it is a shadowy counterpart . . . And modern politics, so far as I am concerned, are those habits and manners of political conduct and reflection which began to emerge in the fifteenth century and to which our current habits and manners are joined by an unbroken pedigree' (pp. 1–2).

xvi

equally modern. They emerged coevally and developed over the past five centuries, constituting the intellectual structure of modern political life which, in practical terms, has been a continual dispute over whether the unprecedented power for control, increasingly available and attractive, to governments should be dispersed or aggregated to achieve 'minute and comprehensive control of all activities'.[17]

Oakeshott, of course, described himself as a sceptic, 'one who would do better if only he knew how'.[18] In the present work, he expresses more fully and poetically that:

> [The] disturbed vision of the weakness and wickedness of mankind and the transitoriness of human achievement, sometimes profoundly felt (as in Donne and Herbert), sometimes philosophically elaborated (as in Hobbes, Spinoza and Pascal), sometimes mild and ironical (as in Montaigne and Burton), was, when it turned to contemplate the activity of governing, the spring of a political scepticism . . . which detracts from the allure of the gilded future foreseen in the vision of faith.[19]

In practice, the politics of scepticism is not identical to philosophical scepticism which is sceptical about the politics of scepticism as well as the politics of faith. The animating spirit of each kind of politics encounters its 'nemesis' whenever the urge to an unmitigated expression of its pure or ideal form takes over. The politics of faith is ever susceptible to the latest plans for improved Towers of Babel; the politics of scepticism too readily devolves into mere playing by the rules of the game, denying the extraordinary.

To advance beyond this ambiguous legacy of 'faith' and 'scepticism' would demand wisdom and insight Oakeshott does not think we can attain. There is little to be gained by pushing to the extreme one ideal or the other, and there is an enormous risk: the misfortune of seeing the present 'as an interlude between night and day', and thus only as an 'uncertain twilight'.[20] The extremes imply that the abstract form of either ideal corresponds to a latent order concealed within, distorted by, or

---

[17] (p. 92).
[18] 'Political Education', in *Rationalism in Politics*, 1962 edn, p. 111; 1991 edn, p. 44.
[19] (pp. 75–6).
[20] (p. 99).

expected to come to pass in and through action in history.[21] But history has no ideal pattern and no end state, either inevitable or willed to be. Those who pursue such things will always be foiled in the effort to put them into practice, and will cause a lot of pain in the process.

If the politics of faith overestimates the possibilities for human action, the politics of scepticism will underestimate or fail to recognize them. Neither the politics of faith nor the politics of scepticism can comprehend the whole of politics. The assertion of the one evokes the counter-assertion of the other, continually recreating the field on which we must operate.[22] We cannot devise any simple principles or propositions to master the complex field of action in which we are situated. Thus politics, in Oakeshott's now famous formulation, is 'the pursuit of intimations'.[23] What is needed, then, is the trimmer: the one who understands the political tradition comprehensively, not chafing at its constraints, yet willing to consider new possibilities.

There is no mistake-proof manner of deciding what should be done. We cannot know that because we have managed to get through one situation we shall do well (or not so well) in the next. This is true for all practitioners, whether informed by the politics of faith or by the politics of scepticism. The advantage of the sceptic is the modest one that the sceptic may make fewer mistakes by not forgetting that politics cannot ever transcend the pursuit of intimations.[24] The sceptical disposition is more open to the contingencies of the human condition manifest in history, its recollective function suggesting sobriety when others are exuberant. 'In the politics of faith,' Oakeshott says,

[21] To seek the fitting middle ground is Oakeshott's practical counsel, not his relentless, subversive, philosophic engagement to dissect the alternatives without concern for what their practitioners may or may not do.

[22] Oakeshott, even at a time when many took him to be at his most political (because, it is said, he was disturbed by the rise of the British Labour Party), was theorizing the whole of modern politics, not just local, current British manifestations.

[23] 'Political Education', in *Rationalism in Politics*, 1962 edn, pp. 124–5; 1991 edn, pp. 57–8

[24] Oakeshott means that politics *cannot* not be the pursuit of intimations. The 'politics of faith' is not an escape from the unavoidability of pursuing intimations, but a misunderstanding and often a self-deception. What inhibits moderation is the immense power available in modernity, and the failure to have obviated war and international conflict which put governments into continual states of emergency.

political decision and enterprise may be understood as a response to an inspired perception of what *the* common good is, or it may be understood as the conclusion which follows a rational argument; what it can never be understood as is a temporary expedient or just doing something to keep things going.[25]

Whereas, the politics of scepticism,

> (regarded as an abstract style of politics) may be said to have its roots either in the radical belief that human perfection is an illusion, or in the less radical belief that we know too little about the conditions of human perfection for it to be wise to concentrate our energies in a single direction . . . to pursue [perfection] as the crow flies . . . is to invite disappointment and . . . misery on the way.[26]

In short, governing by political scepticism, leaves us important matters to attend to but no comprehensive purpose. Nor does such a government claim to be in charge of a preferred manner of living it feels entitled to encourage at the expense of alternatives. The aim is not to tell people how to live, but to maintain arrangements within which people can safely pursue the remarkable multiplicity of imaginable possibilities that human beings, left to their own devices, will bring forth. Thus 'the sceptic understands order as a great and difficult achievement never beyond the reach of decay and dissolution'.[27] This is order in the sense of a framework of rights, duties and means of redress, constituting what Oakeshott calls a 'superficial order'.

By 'superficial order' Oakeshott means a formal arrangement overlaying a deeper, more comprehensive array of human relations which lives and moves and has its being apart from any governmental design, and which no government will ever fully

---

[25] (p. 27).

[26] (p. 31) Scepticism 'considered abstractly' is what sceptics might say if called upon to offer a self-conscious defence of their position, as opposed to taking it for granted. The politics of faith may be carried on by individuals whose 'inspired perception' of the common good is not philosophically reflected upon. Oakeshott's is a limited intervention, not intended directly to alter practices. Specific actions do not follow from philosophic reflection, and conduct is always specific. If practitioners on either side were to take up his analysis and connect it to their specific views and actions, they would do so by their own lights.

[27] (p. 32).

comprehend or subdue. The principal task of the superficial order is to maintain the deeper order and to 'improve' it in the sense of adjusting its explicit arrangements as changing circumstances seem to require. The sceptic, Oakeshott said, thinks of government 'like garlic in cooking ... [to be] so discreetly used that only its absence is noticed'.[28] Governing is interminable because the superficial order:

> has never been designed as a whole, and such coherence as it possesses is the product of constant readjustment of its parts to one another ... the system of superficial order is always capable of being made more coherent. To meditate upon this system and by replying to its intimations to make it more coherent is a manner of improving it which belongs (as the sceptic understands it) to the office of government ... the barbarism of order appears when order is pursued for its own sake and when the preservation of order involves the destruction of that without which order is only the orderliness of the graveyard ... The modest governor in this style does not consider himself better able than his neighbour to determine a general course of human activity.[29]

This, then, is an essay against political excess and the barbarism of perverted order. It is an assessment of the politics and doctrines of the twentieth century which have produced many graveyards of orderliness. And it is an admonition – a call to remembrance – to those polities where the sceptical disposition remains a resource for deliberation. It asks us to travel a while outside the cave of policy preoccupations, to re-acquaint ourselves with the terrain of a more considered understanding of politics. The politics of faith in our day often seems to be more a lament for the loss of vision, and about ineluctable division of purpose, than a celebration of promise fulfilled. If we wish to gain greater understanding of why this should be so, we might well begin here.

---

[28] (p. 36).
[29] (pp. 34–5).

INTRODUCTION

I

For one who speaks neither as a philosopher nor as an historian and whose knowledge of affairs is no more intimate than the low average of his fellows – for such a person to speak about politics requires an apology. The philosopher may find in this field a variety of problems on which we are glad to hear his reflections; from the historian we may learn of the manner in which those changes which we call the political experience of a society have come about; the man of affairs may often have some revealing information to impart or comment to make: each, from his different standpoint, may be expected to have something relevant to say, and between them (apart from what a few specialists may contribute) to compose the total of what may relevantly be said. But to speak informally, in no manner in particular, would appear to be both dangerous and profitless: dangerous, because it lacks the discipline of a technique; profitless, because we may gather from it a harvest and yet not know what to do with the proceeds. Nevertheless, this is the manner in which I propose to speak. And leaving what I have to say to defend itself and to find its own level of usefulness, I shall seek escape from an absolute informality by setting myself some arbitrary limits.

First, I shall be concerned only with modern politics. Some features of modern politics no doubt have their counterpart elsewhere: in the ancient world, for example. But it is a shadowy counterpart, and I propose to venture on no comparisons with what is, in detail, incomparable with our manner of political conduct and reflection. 'Modern history', says Lord Acton, 'tells how the last four hundred years have modified the medieval conditions of life and thought.' And modern politics, so far as I am concerned, are those habits and manners of political conduct and reflection which began to emerge in the fifteenth century and to which our current habits and manners are joined by an unbroken pedigree. This gives us a long period of time over which to range; but not too long. Generally speaking, the vice of contemporary political reflection is to take an excessively long view of the future and an excessively short view of the past. We seem to have got into the habit of thinking that what is significant (whether we like it or deplore it) in current politics dates from the French Revolution, or from 1832 or 1640, and this is an unfortunate habit because by abridging the pedigree of our political character we restrict our understanding of it.

Secondly, as is already apparent, I shall be concerned with the modern politics of Western Europe, and in particular with British politics. It is a time when the mannerisms, if not the manner, of our political pursuits and beliefs have become spread about the world, so that it is now difficult to discern more than a single (though internally complex) political character: political enterprises and expectations (differing, no doubt, in detail) are everywhere more closely assimilated to one another in a more uniform habit of political reasoning than they used to be. And what is available everywhere would seem as well observed in one place as in another. But since this uniformity of character is not only still imperfect and in some respects illusory, but (where it exists) is the product of evangelism and not indigenous growth, we may expect to study the character more profitably where it was born and bred than where (as an adopted character) it is liable to be imperfectly at home.

Thirdly, I shall not be concerned with every aspect of our political pursuits and beliefs, but with one of their aspects – with government, the activity of governing and being governed. If one were considering medieval politics, this would be an absurd restriction of interest, but it is characteristic of the communities of modern Europe to be capable of analysis into rulers and subjects, the rulers being always less numerous than the subjects. This, indeed, is, for us, one of the distinguishing marks of a political community, and it does not depend at all on the enjoyment of any particular form of constitution. Moreover, whatever else belongs to the office of ruler, to be authorized to exert power over the subject is intrinsic to it. The activities of the members of a political community are not, of course, exhausted in the exercise of power by government and the practice of submission by the subject, and there are other ways than this of regarding a society of this sort. But this is a feature of all political communities, and it is this feature I propose to consider. I shall be concerned with the activities of governing and being governed and with the thoughts which compose our understanding of these activities.

But further, these thoughts have, in general, been concerned with two different but related aspects of government: they have been concerned with the question, Who shall rule and by what authority? and with the question, What shall government (composed and authorized in whatever manner we think proper) do? And it is our thoughts about the second of these questions that I propose, mainly, to consider.

The modern history of European politics has most frequently been composed with attention fixed on the first of these questions. It has, consequently, been represented as the story of the changes which have come about in our practices and thoughts about the constitution and authorization of government. And this story has been told so often and so eloquently that we are near to being persuaded that it is the whole story. The assumption which inspired this direction of attention seems to have been the belief that the pursuits of government derive directly from the constitutions of government, and that to have settled the one question is to have decided the other. But a little observation and reflection will tell us that this is not so: there is no simple and direct relation to be discerned between the constitution and pursuits of government. We may have to consider such relation as has revealed itself from time to time, but my main concern will be with the other side of the history of modern government, with our practices and thoughts in regard to the exercise of power by government – not to tell it as an historian would tell it, but to reflect and comment upon it.

These, then, are the limits of our study. It is clear that in modern times governments have become accustomed to doing and attempting what in other times they neither did nor attempted. And it is clear also that what we have become accustomed to think they ought and ought not to do is not merely what has always been thought. The modern world reveals a character of its own in both these respects. My purpose is to explore this character. And although my method is to be informal, there are some precise questions to which I want to find answers: What is the generation and character of the practice of governing in the modern world? How has this practice been understood? What is the generation and character of our thoughts about the proper office of government? And in trying to answer these questions I shall try to show the connection between them.

But first I must explain the distinction I have drawn between the practices and the understanding of the practices of governing, for it is a distinction of investigation rather than of principle. A government may exert itself to do certain things: Henry VIII may dissolve the English monasteries; a twentieth-century cabinet may protect certain industries from foreign competition. From one point of view these are merely events, dissolution and protection. And from this point of view all we can know about them is the same sort of thing as we can know about an earthquake or a plague, namely, their course and, if we persevere very greatly, some of the modifications and displacements they have been partners in bringing about. But the events we are concerned with are not mere events; they are human actions. And as human actions, understanding them is knowing how to interpret them. But by 'interpretation' I do not mean discovering something that lies outside the world of activity, discovering (for example) what was 'in the mind' of the ruler before he performed the action, or discovering his 'motives' or even his 'intentions': these are all unnecessarily complicated and misleading ways of describing what we do when we try to elucidate an action. The characteristic of actions is not that they are preceded by 'decisions' or 'intentions', which may be obscure and have to be unearthed, but simply that they cannot be understood singly. And knowing how to read an action, knowing what it means, interpreting it, is considering it in its context, a context composed entirely of other actions. And until we have understood it in this way we do not know what it is. For example, the dissolution of the monasteries may be read as an action to raise revenue for the Crown, or as a move to extirpate religious error; protection may be understood as increasing prosperity, or as a move to make the country more ready and able to withstand a siege even at the expense of prosperity. And each, understood in one way rather than another, becomes a different action, not because something called its 'intention' is different, but because it is seen to belong to a different context of activity. It is wise, then, to distinguish the actions of government from the understanding of them, not because the understanding of them requires us to go below their surface, but because the actions can be read in various manners, they can belong to diverse contexts, and unless we distinguish we may be misled. On the other hand, this is not a distinction of principle, because the quality of an action, what it is, cannot be separated from the action itself and what we have to investigate is not two things (the action and its meaning) but one thing, namely, the concrete character of the action in its context of activity.

Now, when we ask ourselves the question, What is proper to the office of government? we cannot (if the question is answerable) be considering mere events or the results of events. Events merely happen; they have no propriety. And the results of events are always unascertainable for, though some of the modifications and displacements they help to bring about may perhaps be perceived, there is no reason why we should believe these to be more significant than others which remain obscure, or indeed significant at all, and there is no means of determining the exact contribution of each event to the observed displacement. In this question of propriety, what we are trying to make up our minds about is the propriety of actions performed or to be performed by rulers. And since we cannot judge the propriety of these actions until we know what they are, our beliefs about what is proper to the office of government are beliefs about the propriety of actions read or interpreted in a particular manner. In short, we are concerned, in this question of propriety, not with actions taken singly (that is, with actions whose meaning or character remain undetermined) but with actions in their context of activity.

It is sometimes suggested that our thoughts and beliefs about what is proper to the office of government can be and are premeditated in advance of our experience and understanding of government. And no doubt there is this much truth in the suggestion – that these thoughts and beliefs dimly reflect ideas we may have about propriety in human conduct generally. But these will not, I think, carry us very far: at least they have only a very limited relevance to the ideas current in the modern world about what is proper to the office of government. These general ideas about human conduct are concerned with the behaviour of individual subjects in their relation to one another, and if anything is generally true about our understanding of government in modern times, it is that, unlike the Middle Ages, we observe a distinction between the office and the person, and what we would regard as improper in the person we do not necessarily regard as improper in the office. Nobody thinks that the relations between government and the subject are on all fours with the relations between subject and subject. The grounds and the generation of this distinction we may leave for later consideration, but since the distinction is universally observed in modern times, we must suppose that our thoughts and beliefs about what is proper to the office of government are composed out of what we think can be achieved by the exercise of governmental power, of what we observe to be currently attempted or achieved by governments, qualified by what we are accustomed to expect will be attempted or not attempted and by our current beliefs about the proper directions and objects of human activity. And any vagueness which may remain in this account of the generation of our beliefs about what is proper to the office of government will I hope be dispelled as we go.

Now, since we are to consider our manner of understanding the activity of government and our thoughts about what is proper to the office of government, there is one further question to be settled: Where are we to look in order to catch sight of the object we wish to examine? There are, I think, three sources of information to which we may go. We may hope to elicit what is believed about these things in the modern world from observing what has been and is currently attempted or achieved by governments, from observing the manner in which we are in the habit of talking about the activity of governing, and from considering the writings of men who, from time to time, have disclosed their thoughts on this subject.

These three sources – practice, talk and considered writing – are not, of course, independent of one another, but while it is our exaggeration to say that talk always follows practice and considered writing always springs from talk, there is, as I hope to show, an important sense in which practice is primordial. By practice I mean the pattern of political activity in the modern world. This practice may be fixed in a specific manner of doing things which to a large extent determines what is attempted and what is done; it may, for a time, become more experimental, not unconditioned but conditioned by more general habits of conduct and reflecting changes in habits of conduct; and it may occasionally explain itself in terms of an abstract idea. But whatever its current character, it is the context by means of which we interpret and understand individual actions; and its intelligibility is that of a pattern rather than that of an argument.

Certain kinds of talk may succeed in hardening practice and in making its meaning more obvious; and writing may, on occasion, grind its edge to a sharpness and definition it would not otherwise possess. But while practice and talk unfold themselves candidly and in continuous communication with one another, each elucidating the other, the writings I have in mind are occasional utterances, interruptions in the flow of talk and practice, bearing always the strong impress of an individuality, and are sources of information about the current understanding of the activity of governing, not to be despised, but to be used with appropriate caution.

We long ago learned to be distrustful of medieval speculative writers on politics when our object was to discern what medieval politics were really like, and a similar suspicion is not out of place for modern times. Just as the great formulations of Christian doctrine give an order and subtlety to Christian belief which goes far beyond the piety of, say, a Calabrian peasant or a Chinese convert or indeed the vast majority of believers, and just as a concave mirror will bring together in an exaggerated concentration the scattered objects in a room, so these pieces of political writing often impart to our understanding of the activity of governing a magnified coherence for which we should make allowance. But used with discrimination they may often bring to light what might otherwise remain hidden. If, for example, these writings disclose uncertainty, hesitation or equivocation, we may suppose ourselves to have some evidence of a disharmony of even larger proportions in the less exact understanding which informs the talk and activity of every day. It may be said, then, that of these three sources of information about our understanding of government and our ideas about what is proper to the office of government – the pattern of practice, talk and considered writing – the first is the most reliable, the second is the most copious and revealing, and the third is the most difficult to interpret.

II

Our starting place, then, is not a simple and precise idea of the office of government or our exact conception of the activities proper to government; we begin with an activity being carried on (the activity of governing) and an experience being enjoyed (the experience of being governed). The activity and the experience provoke talk, and from time to time they are written about at various levels of comprehension.

Now, the first thing to be observed about the activity of governing in modern Europe is that it is not simple, monolithic or homogeneous. It never had any of these qualities, and in the course of time its complexity has increased; it has been 'fed with the milk of many nurses', as the sixteenth-century poet says. And this manifold character of our manner of government is reflected unavoidably in the manner in which we talk about it and the difficulty we have in understanding it.

It may be possible to imagine an activity of governing directed to a single end or a homogeneous system of ends, and disclosing an unmixed character. And history may even reveal societies whose government is, so to speak, pure-bred, although even these would be unlikely to escape complexity. But the politics of the societies we are concerned with, the societies of modern Europe, are not of this sort. Even the politics of ancient Athens disclose a manifold and divided character, and certainly since the fall of the Roman Empire in the West no European society can pretend to have enjoyed any but mixed political institutions: their generation has been hybrid, and the diversity of their origin is represented in an absence of homogeneity in their character, which points not in one direction, but in many. And not only are what may perhaps be called the political systems of Europe (those agglomerations of institutions which compose the political behaviour of a people) complex, but each of the institutions which make up each of these systems is itself hybrid in generation and mixed in character.

For example, what we speak of as the institution of kingship in medieval England (which means how kings were accustomed to behave and what was thought about how they ought to behave) is, in fact, an alloy of Anglo-Saxon kingship, feudal overlordship, Christian belief, with an injection at a later stage of the Roman Imperial manner and a dozen other ingredients, none fitting with any exactness to any of the others and each itself already complex in character. Or again, the representative institutions of modern Europe are not only various, but each of them is a mongrel whose pedigree displays contributions from a great variety of sources and whose operation daily bears witness to their heterogeneous origin. And the same, of course, is true of European legal systems; none is pure-bred, each is a miscellany. In short, the habits and institutions which compose our manners of governing are neither rational unities, nor fortuitous collections, but historic compounds.

For this reason, if for no other more philosophic reason, it is dangerously misleading to regard any of our political institutions as instruments designed to serve a specific purpose. A political institution, no matter how heterogeneous its origin, may, at a particular time, be perceived to perform some specific and useful purpose; it may enable us to do something we wish to do or to prevent something happening which we are glad to avoid. But to attribute this function to it as the purpose it serves is, at best, a loose manner of speaking: its purpose, if it can be said to have one, is its place in the system, and there is scarcely any limit to the displacements which would follow the removal of any important political institution. And moreover, to think of it as designed to fulfil this purpose is a gross error. In fact no political institution of any significance was ever designed to fulfil a purpose, or was ever in this sense designed at all. When speaking of political institutions, then, the language of the necessary and the sufficient is wholly inappropriate. And it is the hetero-geneous origin and mixed character of the political institutions of modern Europe which make them eligible for such a variety of uses and eligible also for such a diversity of interpretation.

But it is not only the habits and institutions of modern Euro-pean government which are alloys composed of diverse ele-ments; the language, the political vocabulary in which we speak of the activity of government and make it intelligible to our-selves, is also hybrid. It is a modern language, and like all modern languages it is an amalgam of words and expressions (derived from diverse sources), each of which is in turn a com-plex world of diverse meanings. There are no simple expressions in our political vocabulary, and there are few words which have not done duty, over a period of many centuries, in a great variety of circumstances; and each circumstance, each context, has implanted some special meaning which it is thereafter difficult to exclude. The few words and expressions of recent appearance have all rapidly acquired a complexity of meaning to match that of their fellows in the vocabulary: 'Fascism' is not less multiple than 'democracy' or than 'government' itself. We do not possess a 'scientific' political language in which each expression has a fixed, simple and universally recognized meaning; we have only a living, popular language, at the mercy of use and circumstance, in which each expression is susceptible of many interpretations, none of which is without force and significance.

There is, of course, nothing in all this to surprise us. The heterogeneity characteristic of our political institutions and vocabulary is characteristic also of our blood, our religion and our morality: each is a complex, historic alloy, a mixture of heterogeneous and not always congruous elements. We are used to dealing with complexity and know how to handle it, as we know how to handle our modern languages or how to make the most of a variable climate. There are, it is true, those who sigh for simplicity and homogeneity, a sea without tides, seasons without variety, as Tom Paine dreamed of simplicity in politics and Doughty for homogeneity in language. But for ordinary use a mongrel is recognized to have some advantages: it is more adaptable to circumstances and more fertile than a thoroughbred, and it takes less looking after.

The mixtures which constitute our political habits and our political language are saved from disintegration by the tensions and stresses which have established themselves between their parts, and in each there is a greater opportunity of internal movement than would be possible without injury in a monolithic structure. Where unity is lacking, harmony is sometimes achieved; and the enterprises pursued are usually the result of a resolution of forces, not the exclusive following of a single impulse. And the exploration of the diverse intimations of a complex political habit may result in the appearance of a variety of styles of political activity (as a variety of styles of writing spring from the pursuit of the diverse intimations of a complex language), each exploiting some special element in the mixture but each friendly to one another in so far as they are, in general, not hostile to the alloy.

Now, an activity of governing which enjoys a diverse inheritance and a complex character is normally in a condition of almost continuous internal movement, not swinging to extremes, but undergoing shifts of emphasis, in this or that direction; it does not have to await external stimulus, and it is not determined in advance to a single direction. Such shifts of emphasis may be unobtrusive and perceptible only in retrospect, or they may be of larger dimensions attracting notice to themselves as they occur. They may be occasioned by a change of circumstance (engagement in war, for example; or a great or sudden accession of power at the disposal of government), or by the appearance of some new manner of activity in the subject (such as the growth of industrialization), or they may spring from nothing more significant than the boredom of standing too long upon one emphasis and the desire for merely a different distribution of weight. *La France s'ennuie* was Lamartine's amateur but not imperceptive diagnosis. One way or another, however, a proper understanding of the concrete manner of governing concerned will find these movements intelligible and not disconcerting; they do not destroy the pattern. And even where the impulse of movement is extraneous, each shift is recognizable as the exploitation of something already intimated and none carries us beyond what is tolerably familiar.

Nevertheless, in every heterogeneous and complex activity of governing there are extremes. Normally, the internal movement does not reach them; indeed, so far from being attracted to them it is usually repelled. But in the end it is these poles which, defining the limits of characteristic movement, protect the identity of the manner of governing. Moreover, these extremes may not only be distant from one another, allowing a generous space for manoeuvre; they may even be specifically opposed to one another, the one forbidding all (or most) of what the other prescribes, or at least warrants. And the existence of such opposed extremes is not disruptive of the manner of governing so long as they are mediated to one another by elements in the mixture which, though they are not themselves extreme, partake in some degree of the character of the extremities. This, indeed, is a common observation: the diversity of human character is immense, but the extremes (the saint and the profligate, for example) are made intelligibly human to us by the space between, being filled, without serious *lacuna*, by characters all of which we have no difficulty in recognizing as human.

Circumstances, however, may arise which push the activity of governing decidedly and over a long period in the direction of one of the extremes of which it is capable. An unqualified movement in one direction is rarely the outcome of design, or at least it is not so in the first place. More often it is the result of negligence: we forget that, in order to make the fire burn a little more briskly, we have pulled out all the dampers, and in our enjoyment of the warmth we fail to remark that the scuttle is empty and the chimney near to being on fire. But so long as manifest disaster does not overtake us, we may come to accommodate ourselves to living at an extreme, and we may even fall in love with it: having found ourselves there by chance we may prolong our stay by choice. It is an enticing experience; not to exploit its possibilities seems unreasonable. But in the course of time our understanding of the activity of government contracts to our practice of the activity, our expectations conform to our experiences and our beliefs are assimilated to our situation. For living at an extreme is an insidious pursuit; we may perhaps escape imprisonment in the particular extreme we have come to inhabit, but we are rapidly deprived of the power to recognize anything but an extreme of some sort. As those who pursue high summer round the world think only that they are escaping winter, and forget that they relinquish also the intervening seasons, so those who embrace an extreme in politics come to understand only a politics of extremes. And further, when we have settled at one of the extremes of political activity and have lost touch with the middling region, we not only cease to recognize anything that is not an extreme, but we also begin to confuse the extremes themselves. The poles, which have hitherto been held apart, embrace one another. And our language slips under our feet, becoming equivocal, as it does when an Englishman in search of the sun speaks of *wintering* in Bermuda.

This, then, is the general character of what I have chosen to call the ambiguity which may overtake a manner of political activity; and it is this that I propose to investigate. But already we may observe the general conditions of its appearance. Only a heterogeneous and complex manner of political activity is liable to become ambiguous; and the potentiality is realized when, in such a manner of politics, we cease to exploit its manifold character and come, by circumstance or design, to settle upon an extreme and to recognize only extremes. I have suggested, further, that what I have called modern politics (the activity and the understanding of government in the last five hundred years) is heterogeneous and complex and consequently must be supposed to be liable to be overtaken by ambiguity. Our next step is to consider the evidence in order to determine whether or not there is *prima facie* ground for believing that in our case the potentiality has been realized.

III

Now ambiguity, properly speaking, is a confusion of meanings and is a characteristic of language; its counterpart in conduct is ambivalence, a hovering between two opposed manners or directions of activity. Frequently, I believe, ambiguous talk is the offspring of ambivalent conduct: when our activity is distracted by conflicting pursuits it becomes appropriate to speak in equivocal language. Nevertheless, I think it would be an exaggeration to regard ambivalence as the necessary forerunner of ambiguity; and it is certainly not the cause. An ambiguous vocabulary in use may on occasion cast a spell over conduct, it may open the door to an intrusive ambivalence, it may nourish a yet undeveloped ambivalence, or it may even induce ambivalent conduct by itself suggesting discrepant enterprises. But we are not, I think, called upon to settle the question of precedence; one way or another, ambivalence and ambiguity are in business together as partners. Neither can get on very well without the other, and in considering the one we shall be considering the other at the same time. However, we are now concerned with the understanding of the activity of governing which we reveal in our manner of speaking about it: we are concerned in the first place with ambiguity.

Of course, the world is full of ambiguities:
This brittle world, so full of doubleness.

Complexity is always liable to ambiguity, and simplicity everywhere is an imposition which serves its turn but is irrelevant beyond its special world of reference. Sometimes we can detect the spring of ambiguity in a particular complexity: the discrepancy between 'passion' and 'reason' in human character too long bears the formula of a recognized ambiguity in the 'wearisome condition of humanity'. We owe, I think, some of the ambiguity of our moral and religious beliefs (and possibly of our politics also) to Christianity, a religion which, although it has long ago ceased to be an intruder into a current way of living, has never completely assimilated to itself the civilization we enjoy. If the evidences of Christianity, itself complex and pointing in more than one direction, are written large over the world we live in, there are evidences also of other and older beliefs and manners, and their coincidence may become a source of confusion. But, although connections may be discerned between the ambiguities which prevail in different fields of activity, we are now concerned particularly with politics. And the ambiguity of our current political vocabulary is perhaps its most obvious characteristic: it would be difficult to find a single word that is not double-tongued or a single conception which is not double-edged.

Perhaps the most remarkable of the equivocations of our political vocabulary are the words 'war' and 'peace'; in current use they stand almost perfectly for both themselves and their opposites. The ambiguity of 'freedom' was long ago recognized, but 'free' (when applied to a service supplied by government) and 'liberation' (which means both 'setting' free and 'enslaving' or 'destroying') have come to join it. 'Rights' bear a double meaning; and there is scarcely need to pause in order to draw attention to the *double entendre* in 'democracy'. 'Right' or 'left', when used to indicate not parties but manners, are liable to change places, and 'progressive' and 'reactionary' are disposed to catch the common infection. The ambiguity of 'treason' (when not used as a legal term) and 'traitor' reflects an ambivalent allegiance. 'Security' and 'justice' each bear double and opposed meanings. Even so simple a word as 'order' is double-tongued. And the current dilemma in respect of 'toleration' springs largely from the ambiguity of the word.

Now, that we are well aware of this predicament is revealed by the defences we put up against it. The current strategem is to resolve the ambiguity by applying an adjective to the noun. We know that 'freedom' is ambiguous, and consequently we distinguish, for example, between 'political' and 'economic' freedom, and we speak of the 'new' freedom, as Luther in the sixteenth century spoke of 'christian' freedom. To 'justice' and 'security', on occasion, is prefixed the adjective 'social'; we put 'cold' before war when we mean 'peace'; we distinguish between 'eastern' and 'western' and between 'political' and 'economic' democracy. All this is evidence of an anxiety; but it is a subterfuge which adds little to our relief and nothing to our understanding. Huey Long, who seemed about to strike a blow against ambiguity when he said that 'Fascism' might establish itself in the United States of America but that it would have to be called by another name, revealed the modernity of his political vocabulary when the name he suggested was 'democracy'. It is an ironical situation. The greatest gods of ancient Greece each had many names, and the number of his names proclaimed the number and diversity of the powers the god enjoyed; for these gods were manifold characters. With us, on the contrary, our political deities each have a single name, but beneath it is concealed a character not less manifold and often much more diverse.

Outside modern Europe (and those other parts of the world which have copied our manner of speaking and share our predicament) ambiguous political expressions have not been unknown, but usually the confusion has sprung from the meeting of two political vocabularies each itself not greatly given to equivocation. Thus it was possible for the Romans to deprive the Athenians of independence at the same time as they conferred *libertas*: a vexatious situation. But with us equivocation, although it springs from the complexity of our inheritance, is inherent in our own political vocabulary, which at once conceals and displays a native ambiguity.

Moreover, this ambiguity is not new. In the writings of those who have investigated it (and of course I am not the first to do so) it is often represented as the product of contemporary circumstances, though some writers have seen in the French Revolution the occasion of its appearance. Certainly equivocation has grown upon us, and contemporary circumstances (and not least among them the vast increase of idle political talk) have encouraged its growth; and certainly the French Revolution was something of a landmark in its fortunes. But I think we mistake its character if we do not detect it as something that was already emerging in the sixteenth century, and misunderstand it if we do not interpret it in the context of the whole of modern history. And we miss the *nuance* if we neglect to observe that the French Revolution, that Liberalism, Capitalism, Socialism, Romanticism, Classicism, all these events, processes and movements, which are represented to us as abetting ambiguity by adding new meanings to old words, are themselves ambivalent: none points in one direction only; all are complex and self-divided.

Further, this ambiguity is to be distinguished from a mere corruption of language, and certainly from disingenuous corruption. There cannot be many honest writers on politics who do not from time to time pause to regret that the vocabulary they are obliged to use is so deeply equivocal, and that each word as it comes to the pen is so subtly implicated in considerations they would like to exclude but have no means of excluding: nouns which have become worthless on account of their overcomplication and excessive wealth of meaning, and adjectives ('liberal', 'social') which have gone the way of the nouns. And at these moments we are apt to sigh for an earlier age before these complications set in. But it is an illusion to suppose that the expressions which compose our political vocabulary were ever 'simple', to suppose that they have an 'original meaning' which has become debased, or to suppose that if we get rid of the corruption we shall have resolved the ambiguity. No doubt our political vocabulary is corrupt, no doubt its native ambiguity has been used to spread confusion and hide unscrupulousness, and perhaps also hypocrisy (the tribute vice pays to virtue) is the impulse of some of the equivocation in our political speech. But designing 'double-talk' is effective only because it can rely upon a genuine and deep-seated ambiguity in our political vocabulary, and contemporary proficiency in 'double-think' reflects an artless ambivalence in our conduct.

Now, unless my view of things is mistaken, the ambiguities we are to consider have a common ground; they are emblems of a profound division within our manner of governing and within our manner of understanding the activity of government. And in order to make them intelligible we must consider the extremes between which our political activity and understanding have come to fluctuate. These extremes have been variously identified, and we may notice two representative interpretations, each of which has some cogency but neither of which seems to me to go to the root of the matter.

The poles between which in the modern world the activity of government swings, the extremes between which it is distracted, have been identified as anarchy and collectivism:[1] the absence of government and an activity of governing which knows no limit to what it may properly and profitably undertake. The cogency of this diagnosis lies in its selection of genuine and absolute extremes. It is not only a theoretically complete dichotomy, but it has also some historical ground: 'anarchy', in the modern world, has in fact been represented as a doctrine about the activity of governing. But its defect as a diagnosis lies in the theoretical inappropriateness of 'anarchy' as a concept of government, and in the fact that, while many writers have expressed a suspicion of government and have desired to reduce its field of activity to the smallest possible proportions, only a few eccentrics have considered the abolition of government either practicable or desirable. In short, while 'omnicompetent government' may plausibly be represented as both a theoretic and an historic extreme, 'no-government' is neither theoretically nor historically its opposite. *Laissez faire*, except in the minds of the most naive collectivists, has never meant the abolition of government but only its exclusion from certain of its current engagements; and only in a confused manner of thinking can 'anarchy' represent itself as a manner of governing.

The other representative diagnosis of the condition which has as its symptom the ambiguity of our political vocabulary is that pointed to by Sir James Stephen in a passage in which he contrasts 'two different views' of the relation between rulers and

---

[1] G. Lowes Dickinson, *A Modern Symposium*, p. 65.

their subjects which stand side by side in the modern world.[2] In the one view, he says, 'the ruler is regarded as the superior of the subject' and therefore, if not immune from criticism, criticized only reluctantly and respectfully; in the other view, the ruler is regarded as 'the agent and servant' of the subject, and therefore to be directed and, if need be, censured. But here, it will be observed, the extremes disclosed are concerned not so much with the activity of governing as with the authorization of government. Our language and habits of thought about the authorization of government are perhaps as ambiguous as they are about any other subject, and no doubt they fluctuate between extremes of which this is at least a shrewd account. And, as we have already observed, there is a connection (although not a direct connection) between our way of thinking about the authorization of government and about the activity of governing. But we are concerned here with the activity of governing and our thoughts and ways of speaking about the enterprises proper to it, and consequently we must look elsewhere for the extremes between which it vacillates.

As I understand it, the poles of our activity of governing, the extremes (both theoretic and historic) of which the ambiguities of our speech are an emblem, are neither anarchy and collectivism, nor are they concerned primarily with the authorization of government, but are comprised of two opposed styles of politics which I shall call respectively the politics of faith and the politics of scepticism.

It will be my main task to examine this diagnosis of our political situation, to discuss what it means and to draw some conclusions, both theoretical and practical, from it. But I want it to be understood at the outset that in these two expressions – the politics of faith and the politics of scepticism – I suppose myself to be designating at once the poles of an activity and the poles of our understanding of our activity, the extremes (that is) which make intelligible the ambivalence of our conduct in governing and the ambiguity of our political vocabulary. Each, so far as I am concerned, stands for a manner of going about the business and a manner of understanding what we are doing. Moreover, these two expressions stand not merely for theoretic extremes in conduct and understanding, but also for historic extremes: they stand for the poles between which our conduct and understand-

---

[2] *History of Criminal Law in England*, ii. p. 299.

ing, in modern times, has in fact fluctuated. Consequently they must be regarded neither as simple doctrines about the activity of governing nor as fixed conditions in our conduct of government: their historicity involves them in change; each is a process as well as a condition. We must expect both the politics of faith and the politics of scepticism to appear in a variety of versions (defeated by time or by some other opportunity, in one characteristic enterprise, they reappear in another) and to reflect the changing conditions of Europe during the last five hundred years. History is concerned with the variety of versions, analysis with the elucidation of character.

And further, the doctrines, manners of conduct and enterprises for which these two expressions stand do not correspond, either exactly or indeed at all, with any of the more ephemeral or less complete differences of doctrine and practice which are revealed in modern politics. They do not correspond, for example, with the differences exhibited by contemporary or earlier political parties in England or elsewhere, and they do not correspond with rival manners of thinking and speaking about the authorization of governments. Their significance, so far as I am concerned, lies in the fact that they stand, as shorthand expressions, not for the casual differences with which we are familiar because they lie upon the surface and which we are encouraged to take not very seriously because they are always accommodating themselves to one another, but for the nethermost oppositions in modern politics. And it is because, in spite of their opposition to one another, they speak the same language that this language has become ambiguous and our political activity

> A darkling plain
> Swept with confused alarms of struggle and flight,
> Where ignorant armies clash by night.

IV

One thing remains to be settled before we are properly at work: What harvest do we foresee from our investigation? And it is neither foolish nor superfluous to consider in advance the character and the limits of our expectations, for to be on the look-out for a certain sort of answer is one way of getting our questions more firmly before us, and that is something about which no trouble should be spared.

Our problem is, briefly, the question: What is the character of modern politics that makes its practice run to ambivalence and its vocabulary run to equivocation? So far, we have observed the general conditions of ambivalence and ambiguity. And I have, further, proposed an hypothesis: that the poles of modern political activity and understanding are what I have called the politics of faith and the politics of scepticism. This hypothesis has to be put on trial. But I do not expect to be able to establish it, or to demonstrate its truth; rather, what I hope to be able to show is that it is a revealing hypothesis and to lay before you some of what it reveals. I do not suggest that it is the only hypothesis a sensible man might entertain; I suggest only that it is one worth while investigating. This hypothesis has first to be elucidated: we must have clearly before us what we are supposing. And then it must be set to work. In setting it to work we shall be exploring some of the turns and twists of European political thinking during the last five hundred years. Nevertheless, our study will not be history, properly so called; it will be a study of change but without revealing (what alone interests the historian) the mediation of change. There may be some interesting incidental disclosures, but the main result to be expected is a nearer view of some of the hidden articulations of our politics and, I think, a larger sympathy for our political predicament. And if we discover on the way that what appears to be new in our political situation is, in many cases, only a fresh version of a condition of things which has long prevailed, the only inference I shall suggest is that what has been so long with us is not likely suddenly to vanish or to be easily repressed.

Politics at any time are an unpleasing spectacle. The obscurity, the muddle, the excess, the compromise, the indelible appearance of dishonesty, the counterfeit piety, the moralism and the immorality, the corruption, the intrigue, the negligence, the meddlesomeness, the vanity, the self-deception, and finally the futility,

Like an old horse in a pound,

offend most of our rational and all our artistic susceptibilities. For so far as political activity succeeds in modifying the reign of arbitrary violence in human affairs, there is clearly something to be said for it, and it may even be thought to be worth the cost. But, at the best of times, political activity seems to encourage many of the less agreeable traits in human character.

The easiest way to acquire a sympathy for politics is to become a partizan; and there is nothing disreputable in partizanship: indeed, not to take sides lays us open to the appearance of abominable superiority. But there is a sympathy of a less intense but also less vulnerable kind, which springs from allying ourselves with necessity and accepting the unavoidable: the sort of sympathy Spinoza had with the universe. And it is this sort of sympathy, if any, that we may expect to acquire from the kind of investigation I am proposing. Politics, of course, knows nothing of genuine necessities: there is nothing in the world of politics which does not spring from human activity, although there is much that is not a consequence of human design. And with respect to human activity the language of the necessary and the efficient is inappropriate. But since we shall be concerned with those strategic movements in our politics which, because they are exceptionally deep-rooted, are relatively difficult to change, and altogether impossible to redress, we shall be considering what does not require us to take sides: at this level, not to get involved in the current choices is appropriate and not merely superior. We are concerned, then, with a level at which 'things and actions are what they are and the consequences of them will be what they will be', and where the only appropriate ambition is not to be deceived. And to distinguish the more permanent elements of the pattern of our politics, to accept them, not in the degree in which they are acceptable (for that becomes irrelevant) but in the degree in which they are unavoidable, is to find oneself a little less perplexed and a little more understanding of even the unpleasing surface of politics. And if there is any conclusion I wish particularly to avoid, it is the fruitless conclusion that a virtuous politics would seek simplicity and 'shun ambiguous alloy', that what we ought to aim at is a resolution of the ambivalence and ambiguity of our politics or at least a formula under which they can be vanquished.

2

THE AMBIGUITY IDENTIFIED

I

Our starting point is the evident ambiguity of our political vocabulary, an ambiguity which has both merit and defect. Its merit is practical: like a veil which softens the edges and moderates the differences for what it at once hides and reveals, this ambiguity of language has served to conceal divisions which to display fully would invite violence and disaster. Its defect is mainly philosophical: the ambiguity makes it difficult for us to think clearly about our politics and stands in the way of any profound political self-knowledge. And it may be added that the opportunity it gives the disingenuous politician to spread confusion is a practical defect to set against its practical usefulness.

My object is not to denounce the treachery of language, or to resolve or otherwise remove the ambiguity, but to understand it. And the hypothesis I have proposed for examination is that the ambiguity of our political vocabulary springs from the fact that it has been obliged, for nearly five centuries, to serve two masters.

These two masters I have called the politics of faith and the politics of scepticism, expressions which stand for the two poles or extremes between which, in modern times, our activity of governing and our understanding of what is proper to the office of government have fluctuated. As extremes they are ideal: they are the horizons of an activity and an understanding which, for the most part, have occupied less room than the extremes allow. But in so far as activity and understanding are set in the direction of one or other of these ideal extremes, two historic styles of politics appear, the qualities of each being the qualities of the extreme it approaches, modified, of course, by the incompleteness of the approach. During the five centuries of modern history, these two styles of political activity have lain side by side, unobtrusive (save on the notable occasions when one or other has swung particularly close to its theoretic extreme), and, owing to the ambiguity of our political vocabulary, often ill-distinguished from one another. Moreover, since they are styles of political activity, and not fixed, unvarying doctrines, each has appeared not only in varying degrees of completeness, but also in a variety of versions. And by a 'version' of a political style I mean the deployment of the resources of the style in a particular context and in order to bring them to bear upon a particular political situation. Consequently, in any locality and in any period in the history of modern Europe it is possible to detect not only the current intensity of each of these styles of politics (namely, the degree in which there and then they approach their respective ideal extremes), but also the current version of each, that is, the manner in which they are being applied to the current political situation. The analogy of architecture will make my meaning clear. In the activity of building, certain regularities of treatment may be discerned, and by a process of abstraction the ideal principles of a style of architecture may be formulated. It is scarcely to be expected that any single building will represent exactly this ideal style, but a building may be observed to approach it more or less closely. Moreover, the exigencies of the site, or of the available materials, or of the use for which the building is designed may further condition the manner in which it is built. So that we may not only observe the degree in which it approaches to an ideal style, but also detect in it the employment (in some degree or other) of the principles of the style for a special purpose.

Now, we shall be concerned with some of the versions of the two styles to which modern politics has run, not, unfortunately, to trace their emergence and succession in detail (which is the business of the historian), but in order to enlarge our knowledge of the styles themselves by observing their behaviour in different circumstances. But before we begin to consider, in this manner, the historic fortunes of these two styles of politics, we shall be wise to have their abstract principles as clearly before us as may be. We should remind ourselves, however, that these principles *are* abstract; that is, they have been arrived at by a process of abstraction. The materials we have to work upon are whatever we can find out about the manner in which modern European peoples have gone about the business of governing and the understanding they have had (and expressed in words) of the proper office of government. By reflecting upon this we may distinguish what I have called different styles of political activity, and by extrapolating the tendencies which are represented in a style we may formulate the ideal extreme towards which it points.

II

We will consider first the politics of faith; and I think the appropriateness of the expression, which is perhaps not unmixed with paradox, will appear as we go.

In the politics of faith, the activity of governing is understood to be in the service of the perfection of mankind. There is a doctrine of cosmic optimism which, not from observation but as an inference from the perfection of its creator, attributes an unavoidable perfection to the universe. And there is, further, a doctrine in which human perfection appears as a providential gift, assured but not deserved. But the idea of human perfectibility characteristic of the politics of faith, so far from being derived from either of these doctrines, is hostile to them both. In the politics of faith, human perfection is sought precisely because it is not present; and further, it is believed that we need not, and should not, depend upon the working of divine providence for the salvation of mankind. Human perfection is to be achieved by human effort, and confidence in the evanescence of imperfection springs here from faith in human power and not from trust in divine providence. We may, perhaps, be permitted to encourage ourselves by believing that our efforts have the approval and even the support of providence, but we are to understand that the achievement of perfection depends upon our own unrelaxed efforts, and that if those efforts are unrelaxed, perfection will appear.

This first principle is partnered by three others. Perfection, or salvation, is something to be achieved in this world: man is redeemable in history. And it is on account of this belief that it is both relevant and revealing to speak of this style of politics as 'Pelagian'. Further, the perfection of mankind is understood not only to be mundane, but to be a condition of human circumstances. But there is room here for confusion. If human character were thought to be independent or even partly independent of human circumstances, then, of course, it would be proper to exclude the perfection of human character from the pursuits of the politics of faith, and the style would be seen to have some limit to its ambition. But, in general, this is not so. Men, it is believed by those who embrace this style, are the creatures of their circumstances,[1] and consequently their perfection is identified with a condition of those circumstances. And indeed, it is in the end only on account of this identification, which permitted this style of politics to seek all that a man can desire, that it becomes distinguishable from any other style. Finally it is believed that the chief agent of the improvement, which is to culminate in perfection, is government. Thus it comes about that the activity of governing is understood as the control and organization of human activity for the purpose of achieving human perfection.

Now, among these ideas there are several which have an indelibly modernistic appearance, and if these are the roots of the politics of faith it would seem incautious to push its emergence back to the beginning of modern history. Nevertheless, these beliefs have enjoyed a longer history than is often supposed, and although my statement of them is, for the most part, in the confident and adult language of the eighteenth century, they were first hatched at a much earlier date. At a later stage I shall do my best to remove the suspicion that I am attributing an excessively long life to what is often believed to be a very recent appearance, but perhaps the suspicion may for the moment be restrained if we observe two things. First, that what I believe to be the prime condition of the emergence of the politics of faith (namely, a remarkable and intoxicating increase of human power) is characteristic of the beginning of modern history and not merely of recent times; and secondly, that there is room in this style of politics for a variety of interpretations (some of them not at all modernistic) of the keyword 'perfection'. The millennium which is inseparable from this style of politics must, it is true, be a mundane condition of human circumstances, but it may range from a condition of moral virtue or religious salvation to a condition of 'prosperity', 'abundance' or 'welfare'. In short there are versions of this style of politics appropriate not merely

---

[1] An early rationale of this belief was, of course, provided by Locke.

to the circumstances of the eighteenth and nineteenth centuries, but even to those of the sixteenth century.

There are, however, two features of this first sketch of the politics of faith which it is important not to mistake. First, the activity of governing is not understood as merely an auxiliary agent in that pursuit of improvement which is itself perfection or which is to culminate in perfection; it is the chief inspirer and sole director of the pursuit. If the doctrine were merely that the office of government is to contribute some recognizable benefit to mankind, then there would be nothing to distinguish the politics of faith from every other doctrine, except perhaps from a doctrine of anarchism. We must be clear that what we are considering is an understanding of the activity of governing which attributes to government itself (and gives reasons for doing so) the duty and the power to 'save' mankind, although within this style of politics a variety of interpretations of 'salvation' are likely to appear.

The second point concerns 'perfection'. I have said that a millennium is inseparable from this style of politics, and it may be thought that here I am claiming for it so narrow a doctrine as to make it a style which could be attributed to only a few eccentrics, and one insignificant in the broad picture of modern politics. A style of politics which aims at the improvement of human circumstance is something we are all familiar with; perfection is an unusual excess. The distinction, however, is in this connection impossible to maintain. In the politics of faith I am, it is true, delineating what are generally spoken of as utopian politics, but those who try to escape from this by claiming only the pursuit of improvement, not perfection, will I think find this way of retreat too narrow if they wish to carry with them the particular notion of improvement to which they nevertheless cling.

Putting aside, then, the obtrusive millenarians, who are a special class in the ranks of the politics of faith, let us consider the improvers who deny utopian pretensions. The enterprise to improve the lot of mankind may be undertaken in two ways. We may project, appropriate or develop all manner of changes which suggest themselves as changes for the better, 'better' signifying an improved way, other things being equal, of engaging in this or that activity or of enjoying the world in which we find ourselves. Here the improvement of circumstances follows no single direction, and if one improvement conflicts with another (as may very well be the case) then there will be a temporary adjustment between their claims: neither the improvements themselves, nor the adjustments between them, intimate or impose a single track.

The other manner of pursuing the improvement of human circumstances is first to decide upon the direction in which the 'better' lies and to pursue that one direction: how this decision is made does not matter. This assumes not a detailed knowledge of the best, but at least an idea of the best, because the direction selected is chosen, not because it is on the whole better than any alternative, but because it is the best. And it is this manner of pursuing improvement which belongs to the politics of faith. As we shall see, many of the adherents of this style of politics deny that they are perfectionists or utopians, and their denial (if it is not mere self-deception) means something: it means that the condition of things they wish to see established is not exactly predictable in advance and is not expected to come down from heaven to earth ready-made. It does not mean, however, that they have any hesitation about the direction in which improvement is to be sought.

In short, if you posit a single road, no matter how slowly you are prepared to move along it or how great the harvest you expect to gather as you go, you are a perfectionist, not because you know in detail what is at the end, but because you have excluded every other road and are content with the certainty that perfection lies wherever it leads. And the office given to government in this enterprise is appropriate not only because of the amount of power it can exert but also because it needs to be exerted in one direction only.

One of the characteristic assumptions, then, of the politics of faith is that human power is sufficient, or may become sufficient, to procure salvation. A second assumption is that the word 'perfection' (and its synonyms) denotes a single, comprehensive condition of human circumstances. This condition may not readily be established, and we may not be able to premeditate it with any great degree of distinctness, but we can at least discern its general outline; it is the goal of all political activity, and there is no alternative to it. Consequently, this style of politics requires a double confidence: the conviction that the necessary power is available or can be generated, and the conviction that, even if we do not know exactly what constitutes perfection, at least we know the road that leads to it. The confidence that the necessary power is available may be expected to grow with the pursuit of perfection; the confidence that we are on the right road may be acquired in various ways. It may be a visionary certainty, or, alternatively, it may be the fruit of research, reflection and argument. In the politics of faith, political decision and enterprise may be understood as a response to an inspired perception of what *the* common good is, or it may be understood as the conclusion which follows a rational argument; what it can never be understood as is a temporary expedient or just doing something to keep things going. Consequently, in this understanding of politics, the institutions of government will be interpreted, not as means for getting things done or for allowing decisions of some sort to be made, but as means for arriving at the 'truth', for excluding 'error' and for making the 'truth' prevail.

The politics of faith understands governing as an 'unlimited' activity; government is omnicompetent. This, indeed, is only another way of saying that the object in government is 'salvation' or 'perfection'; but saying it in this way enables us to observe an important distinction: the distinction between 'absolutism' and 'omnicompetence'. A doctrine of absolutism, properly speaking, refers to the authorization of government. It implies a governing power which is not indeed self-authorized (for that, though theoretically possible, is unknown to history), but authorized in such a manner that the authorization once given cannot, or cannot easily, be withdrawn, modified, transferred or otherwise interfered with; and perhaps it implies, also, an authorization which bestows all the power appropriate to government upon one person or body of persons who do not share the exercise of it with anybody else. In some significant respects, it seems to me, all governments are, in this sense, 'absolute'. At least, a 'government' whose authorization can be withdrawn as soon as it has been given, on the least pretext or on none at all, and one which is obliged to share its responsibility with persons or bodies which have not received the same or any authorization, seems to me to be qualified in a manner in which most governments in modern times are not in fact qualified. But, be that how it may, all this is something wholly different from an 'omnicompetent' government. Research has disclosed the circumstances in which 'sovereign' government emerged in the modern world; it remains to disclose the circumstances of the emergence of 'minute' government; for though they appear roughly equal, they are by no means the same thing. 'Minuteness' or 'omnicompetence' refers not to the authorization of government, but to the activity and objects in governing. For example, Hobbes may fairly be said to have understood government as the exercise of an 'absolute'

authority, and to be the first great theorist of sovereign government, but he shows no sign (indeed, quite the reverse) of understanding the activity of governing as an omnicompetent activity.
There is absent from his pages any idea whatever of government
as the agent of human improvement and perfection (the idea of
human perfection is for him absurd), and there are present
some very precise and far-reaching ideas about the limited,
though very important, objects appropriate to the activity of
governing. Government is paramount, but its activities are
narrow.

Now, in the politics of faith the activity of governing is understood as properly omnicompetent but not necessarily absolute.
In other words, 'collectivism' of some sort belongs as such to the
politics of faith, but Caesarism (which, it has been well said, left
the Roman Empire 'a happy arena of idiosyncrasy') does not
belong to it in any greater degree than it belongs to all government. The politics of faith understands governing as an endlessly
proliferating activity, integrating all the activities of the subject,
and (if it is faithful to its charge) always at the end of its tether.
And of the many consequences of this feature of the politics of
faith, one should be noticed at once. The words and expressions
of our political vocabulary are each capable of a narrow and an
extended meaning (and, of course, a range of meaning between
these limits). In the politics of faith, because of its alliance with
the enterprise of human perfection, each word and expression
will be given its largest and most extended meaning: it goes
always to the limit, and (by means of adjectives) sometimes
beyond the limit, of what the vocabulary will tolerate without
becoming meaningless.

This sketch of the politics of faith, even when it is taken for
what it is intended to be, an abstract design, is imperfect; but
reflecting upon it, certain obvious inferences present themselves. And to set down briefly a few of them will be a means at
once of amplifying the sketch itself, and of preparing ourselves
for what we are to meet when we turn from abstractions to the
concrete versions of this style of politics in action.

Clearly, it belongs to this style of politics to welcome power
rather than to be embarrassed by it; and no quantity of power
will be considered excessive. Indeed, to brood over every activity,
to keep every enterprise in line, not to be behindhand in
expressing its approval or disapproval of every undertaking, and,
in short, to concentrate all the power and resources of the
community upon the project of perfection, making certain that

none is unexploited or wasted, will obviously be appropriate to the activity of governing understood as the organization of human perfection. Not as a defect but as a virtue, in proportion to the power at its disposal, the activity of governing in this style of politics will be minute, inquisitive, and unindulgent: society will become a *panopticon* and its rulers *panoverseers*. And not inadvertently but unavoidably, this concentration of effort, again in proportion to its power, will constitute government as the representative of the society in an enterprise of communal self-assertion whose purpose will be the spiritual, if not the physical, conquest of the world: to hide the 'truth' would be treachery, to be idle in propagating it, disgrace.

Further, it would appear that a high degree of formality in the activity of governing would be out of character. Governing in this style is a godlike adventure, and a nice observance of rules and constitutions will readily be felt to hinder its impetus. Rights, the means of redress, will be incongruous, their place being taken by a single, comprehensive Right – the right to participate in the improvement which leads to perfection. Precedent will play no great part in this style of governing; the present will be more important than the past, and the future [more important] than either. *Raison d'état*, redeemed and sanctified by its association with the enterprise of perfection, will be recognized as an appropriate, a cogent, even a moralistic argument. Abhorrence of retrospective legislation will be out of place; prevention will be considered better than punishment; that the innocent should suffer will appear less vile than that the guilty should escape, and guilt will more readily be presumed than innocence. Opposition, appropriately understood as a means of arriving at the 'truth', will have only a temporary and sporadic usefulness and will be recognized as a hindrance or worse when the 'truth' is apparent.

Moreover, it will be proper for an activity of governing wedded to the enterprise of perfection to require not merely obedience or submission from the subject, but approval and even love. Dissent and disobedience will be punished, not as troublesome conduct, but as 'error' and 'sin'. Lack of enthusiasm will be considered a crime, to be prevented by education and to be punished as treason. And, on the other hand, this style of governing, with its single-hearted impulse to perfect, may be expected to provoke dissatisfaction, because perfection will lie in the future and we are always more dissatisfied when we lack one thing than when we lack many things. Finally, the office of government will properly achieve a moral elevation which puts it above every other office, the politician and his associates being understood to be at once the servants, the leaders and the saviours of society.

III

Since we are dealing, at present, with abstract extremes, it is proper (and not mere exaggeration) to see in the politics of scepticism (which we may now consider) a style of politics in every respect the opposite of the politics of faith. But there is an error to be noticed and avoided at this point, because if we do not escape it now we shall find it magnified when we come to deal with the historical fortunes of these two styles of politics. I mean the error of converting logical opposites with historical enemies, and here of regarding faith as a reaction against scepticism, or scepticism as a reaction against faith, and understanding them only in so far as they are mirrored in one another. In some respects I think there are versions of the politics of scepticism which antedate any of the politics of faith in the modern world, and there are obvious reasons why this should be so. But since it is my contention that both these styles of politics are present (though not of course at all times equally energetic) from the beginning and throughout modern history, they are, for our purpose, coeval, and it would be out of place to assign precedence to either style. In exposition, one must be taken before the other, but in fact, as we come upon them, they are coincident. My view is that the history of modern politics (in respect of the activity of governing) is a *concordia discors* of these two styles; and I believe that those who see the spring of faith in the failure of scepticism, or the spring of scepticism in the collapse of faith, are mistaken. Of course, intertwined as they have been, they have acted and reacted upon one another, and they have even modified one another (each hindering the other from reaching its theoretic extreme), but the grounds of each lie independently in the circumstances of modern politics. And, as I have said, neither is to be identified with the differences, divisions, antagonisms, alignments and parties which compose the surface of the history of our politics and which exist largely or wholly as they are reflected in one another. We are considering, then, two styles of politics which are in abstract opposition to one another, but which together compose our complex and ambivalent manner of governing and our complex and ambiguous understanding of what is proper to the office of government.

Scepticism at work is never absolute: total doubt is merely self-contradictory. And as a manner of understanding the activity of governing, scepticism is not to be identified with anarchy or the stark individualism which is often the partner of anarchy.[2] On the contrary, in the politics of scepticism governing is understood as a specific activity, and in particular it is understood to be detached from the pursuit of human perfection. Intellectually, this detachment may be achieved either when human perfection is not regarded as a mundane condition of human circumstances, or when the pursuit of perfection is recognized to be proper to mankind but when some other authority than government is thought to be in charge of it. With certain qualifications, this may be said to have been the manner of sceptical politics characteristic of medieval Europe. The detachment of government from the pursuit of perfection may, however, be achieved in other ways; and in modern times the politics of scepticism (regarded as an abstract style of politics) may be said to have its roots either in the radical belief that human perfection is an illusion, or in the less radical belief that we know too little about the conditions of human perfection for it to be wise to concentrate our energies in a single direction by associating its pursuit with the activity of governing. Human imperfection (so the argument runs) may be evanescent, and, moreover, it may be a single and simple condition of human circumstances (though this may be doubted), but, even on these assumptions, to pursue perfection in one direction only (and particularly to pursue it as the crow flies, regardless of what there may be to do in the interval before we embrace it) is to invite disappointment and (what might be worse than the mortification of non-arrival) misery on the way. On the whole, since we are considering modern times, I think it more accurate to find the roots of sceptical politics in this prudent diffidence rather than in some more radical doubt. Radical doubt has not been absent, nor has another view (not touched on here), the view that the pursuit of perfection is far too important to be handed over to the control and direction of a set of people who by blood, force or election have acquired the

[2] Anarchy, historically, has closer affiliations with the politics of faith than with the politics of scepticism. The antinomian tendency of faith is, itself, anarchic at the same time as being tyranous.

right to call themselves 'governors'; but neither radical doubt nor this other correction is necessary for the detachment of the activity of governing from the pursuit of perfection.

This detachment deprives the activity of governing of the comprehensive purpose (the pursuit of the common good) which it enjoys in the understanding of the politics of faith. The office of government here is not to be the architect of a perfect manner of living, or (as faith understands it) of an improved manner of living, or even (as it turns out) of any manner of living at all. But to be deprived of this is not to be deprived of every-thing. And the affirmations which the politics of scepticism makes about the activity of governing will be found, I think, to be based not, like faith, upon a doctrine about human nature, but upon a reading of human conduct. The sceptic in politics observes that men live in proximity with one another and, pursuing various activities, are apt to come into conflict with each other. And this conflict, when it reaches certain di-mensions, not only makes life barbaric and intolerable, but may even terminate it abruptly. In this understanding of politics, then, the activity of governing subsists not because it is good, but because it is necessary. Its chief office is to lessen the severity of human conflict by reducing the occasions of it. And this office may bestow a 'good' in so far as it is performed in a manner which is harmonious with, and does not prejudice, the kind of conduct which is currently approved.

This superficial order may seem insignificant (something that the politics of faith assumes without remarking upon it), and to preserve it may seem a menial occupation. But the sceptic under-stands order as a great and difficult achievement never beyond the reach of decay and dissolution. He has what Henry James called 'the imagination of disaster', and consequently he re-minds us that even superficial order is as fragile as it is valuable and that when it collapses life rapidly becomes 'solitary, poor, nasty, brutish and short', with no opportunity at all for pursuing perfection and little for contemplating it. But although this superficial order is not to be despised, it is not everything. Con-sequently it falls to the sceptic to insist that we shall do well not to spend upon it more of our resources than is necessary for its preservation.

Now, the expense it entails is the concentration of what at the best of times will be a large quantum of the power available in the community and is the seconding of human activity from more agreeable pursuits. Weak government is useless. And in the understanding of the sceptic strong government is not to be confused with a step in the direction of the politics of faith because it is not to be confused with minute government: its strength is always qualified by the narrow range of its activity. But, be this as it may, it is clearly in character for the sceptic to consider economy in the use of power in governing, and most of our practices and ideas in this matter spring from this style of politics. We are not at present concerned with these practices and ideas themselves which belong properly to the various versions of the politics of scepticism, but it is relevant even in the abstract design to observe the appropriateness, in the interests of economy, of the conduct of government (that is, the maintenance of order) by means of known and settled laws and a system of rights which is bound up with (which, indeed, is historically derived from) known and easily operated means of redress. This manner of governing is at least more economical in its use of power than what is, in general, the only possible alternative – the continuous or sporadic interruption of human activities by *ad hoc* corrective measures requiring not a steady and moderate pressure in the direction of order, but the constant mobilization and demobilization of great quantities of power. But the point of principle here is that, in the understanding of the sceptic, the activity of governing is a *judicial* activity, and the power which is concentrated in the office of government is not available to anyone who has a favourite project to promote or impose.

Moreover, there is another reason why it is appropriate for the sceptic to be specially concerned with the economy of power in government. Starting, theoretically, from a reading of human conduct which expects human conflict, and seeing no way of abolishing it without abolishing much else at the same time, the sceptic is not disposed to forget that the office of government is occupied by men of the same make as the subjects they rule – men, that is to say, who are always liable, when they become governors, to go beyond their terms of reference and impose upon the community an 'order' particularly favourable to their own interests, or (in an excess of generosity or ambition) to impose something more than order. And on this account, also, it is appropriate for the politics of scepticism to be sparing of the quantity of power invested in government. And if it turns out to be necessary to second more human activity in order to constitute a body, not of governors but of custodians of government, this will be counted as part of the unavoidable cost of good government, a cost nevertheless to be kept at the most economical level.

In the sceptical understanding of governing, then, the maintenance of order is the first object of government. But there is what appears to be a second object: to seek out improvements, and where appropriate to improve the system of rights and duties and the concomitant system of means of redress, which together compose the superficial order. This activity of 'improvement' is, of course, to be distinguished from the improvement which in the politics of faith is understood to be the comprehensive purpose in government. Here what is to be improved is not human beings, or the conduct of human beings, or even in a broad way human circumstances, but the existing system of rights, duties and means of redress. And the directions in which improvement is to be sought are unmistakable: some are more radical than others, but none carries the activity of governing away from its first object. Indeed, 'improvement' here is merely part of the articulation of maintaining order.

It will be observed that both the manner of maintaining order and the character of the order itself will always be conditioned by the sort of activities which members of the community are engaged in. These activities are liable to change. Indeed, in modern European communities they change continuously: every one of the thousands of mechanical inventions has brought about a change of this sort. In this understanding of politics, the business of government is not to determine what these activities shall be, but to guard against their becoming disruptive of that order without which all activity (except of the most primitive or unrewarding kind) is impossible. And to pursue the current changes in activity with the necessary adjustments in the system of rights, duties and means of redress is the most radical form of improvement of which government, in this style of politics, is capable. It will be noticed, however, that this activity of 'improvement' is not an independent activity additional to the activity of maintaining order; it is itself the maintenance of an appropriate order. To neglect it is not to leave undone a supplementary duty; it is precisely to allow disorder to institute itself. And on this account the activity of improvement is not, strictly speaking, a second object of government; it is merely an aspect of the first and only object.

But further, every system of rights, duties and means of redress is internally in a state of disequilibrium. The system has never been designed as a whole, and such coherence as it possesses is the product of constant readjustment of its parts to one another. And even if no change in the direction of activities took place, the system of superficial order is always capable of being made more coherent. To meditate upon this system and by replying to its intimations to make it more coherent is a manner of improving it which belongs (as the sceptic understands it) to the office of government, although he will be suspicious of a great love of symmetry and an overbearingly eager impulse to abolish anomalies.

Other appropriate directions of improvement are even more obvious. The activity of governing may always be made more economical in its use of power and resources; and there will always be room for the sort of improvement which makes the order less onerous without making it less effective. It will be clear gain if a smaller amount of human activity is diverted into the unprofitable occupation of circumventing some excess of order or of seeking out some cranny in which to escape the frustration imposed by a too insistent orderliness. For the sceptic, there is a barbarism of order no less to be avoided than the barbarism of disorder; and the barbarism of order appears when order is pursued for its own sake and when the preservation of order involves the destruction of that without which order is only the orderliness of the ant-heap or the graveyard.

The activity of governing, then, as the sceptic understands it, belongs to a complex of activities; it is one among a hundred others and it is superior to the whole complex only in respect of being the activity of overseeing all from the standpoint of public order. Government is not the imposition of a single moral or other direction, tone, or manner upon the activities of its subjects. The range and direction of activity in the community are what they are, and within it, of course, is the activity of moral approval and disapproval of current conduct. But moral approval and disapproval are no part of the office of government, which is not at all concerned with the souls of men. Who is right and who is wrong, in any ultimate sense, is not decided and does not need to be decided; nor is it necessary to invoke a speculative theory of sacrosanct individualities (such as J. S. Mill's doctrine of liberty) or (on the other hand) of social solidarity; the sole concern of government is the effect of conduct upon public order. The modest governor in this style does not consider himself better able than his neighbour to determine a general course of human activity. But there his diffidence ends: in his narrow business he can afford to be inexorable. It is to keep in working order the means of redress to which those who have been denied their rights can have recourse, to see that these rights and duties are appropriate to the current condition of the society, and to prevent corruption of this 'justice'. And if we add to this the task of taking thought for the protection of the community against a foreign foe, and of defending its interest (if it has any) in the world at large, we are adding nothing new. It is true that this order guardianship has to be exercised in a more empirical manner and is less a matter of enforcing rights and duties than of pursuing policy; but its limits are the same, and to lead a moral crusade against a foreign country is as much out of character in this style of governing as to lead a moral crusade against any of its subjects. In short, in the politics of scepticism, government is like good humour and raillery; the one will not get us to heaven and the other does not demonstrate 'truth', but the first may save us from hell and the second from folly.

Now, as with the politics of faith, we may fill in this abstract design of the politics of scepticism by considering a few of its implications. It is appropriate in this style of government and understanding of the activity of governing that there should be a certain nervousness about the exercise of power: where the limits are severe the liability to overstep them, inadvertently or ambitiously, is great. I do not think we need attribute to the sceptic in politics anything like a belief, as a matter of principle, in the absolute value of variety in human conduct; rather, he observes that such variety exists and does not conceive himself or anybody else to have the authority to destroy it. Nevertheless, government is taking a certain control over the conduct of all the inhabitants of a territory; and in order to perform its narrow task, it unavoidably finds itself in possession of power which, if used for the purpose, is sufficient to impose a more extensive uniformity than is required for the maintenance of superficial order. Consequently, the characteristic defect of the virtue of this style of government will be not weakness on the occasion, but a tendency to understate the occasion. Believing that, like garlic in cooking, government should be so discreetly used that only its absence is noticed, the suspicions of the sceptic are at once aroused by obtrusive activity. Nevertheless, he is in no doubt that the absence of government would be noticed.

Further, in this style of governing a high degree of formality will be appropriate, and there will be considerable attention paid to precedent. But this will not be on account of any belief that precedent represents 'truth' and that to depart from it is 'error', but merely because if the maintenance of order is not itself orderly it will rapidly degenerate into partiality or the pursuit of favourite projects. Formality is valued by the sceptic because it is an inexpensive manner of avoiding excess in a matter where defect is preferable to excess. Similarly, in the sceptical style of politics retrospective legislation and any torturing of the laws in order to penalize conduct which is not clearly proscribed will be out of character; punishment will be definite and will be reserved for those convicted of crime in one or other of its known degrees; the barbarous verdict of 'not proven', the relic of clannish intransigence masquerading in the garments of scientific accuracy, which belongs to the politics of faith, will have no place. And so far as the conduct of the individual subject is concerned, punishment will be preferred to prevention because, in general, it is impossible to prevent an action without taking control over a large area of the conduct which surrounds it and without the exercise of great power – without, in short, turning civil society into a badly managed classroom in which every lesson is preceded by a search for catapults, cribs and chess sets, a search which makes pupils and teachers equally miserable and anxious for the holidays.

And again, the sceptic's belief that governing is not a matter of establishing the 'truth' of a proposition and of translating the proposition into conduct, but is a matter of enforcing a certain superficial order, will determine him in his understanding of some of the familiar institutions of modern government. Discussion and 'opposition' will not be regarded as means for 'the discovery of truth',[3] but as means for calling attention to something that might otherwise have been forgotten and for keeping government within its proper bounds, and consequently they will be activities not to be resorted to occasionally and reluctantly but continuously. And, in general, the sceptic will value most highly not those aspects of institutions which make them apt to dispatch business, but those aspects which diminish the damage that may be done when they are in the hands of ambitious men. He recognizes that, however limited the sphere of government, it will always be an activity for which human beings are not fully qualified: it demands a disinterestedness which is always absent.

[3] Lindsay, *Essentials of Democracy*, p. 35.

And consequently, in certain circumstances he will welcome 'corruption' if it is the means of countering more serious partiality or more devastating ambition.

Finally, in the politics of scepticism the activity of governing is manifestly nothing to be enthusiastic about, and it does not demand enthusiasm for its services. The rulers will occupy an honoured and respectable, but not an elevated, place; and their most notable qualification will be that they claim no godlike capacity for directing the activities of their subjects – *dis te minorem quod geris imperas.*[4]

IV

With the abstract design of these two styles of politics before us, my contention that the ambivalence of modern politics is a distraction of both activity and understanding which has these as its poles begins to take shape. Here the two manners of conducting and of understanding government are starkly opposed to one another because they are the abstract extremes of which our politics are capable. But, of course, abstract extremes are ideal; historically our practice and our understanding of government has occupied a middle region with only sporadic excursions to the horizons. Nevertheless, both practice and understanding have looked and moved in both directions; and these glances and movements have constituted our two styles of politics.

Now, it would appear that these two styles are, in their extremes, so radically opposed to one another that communication between them is not to be expected: what one asserts the other denies, and only when, in the middle region, a certain common self-forgetfulness supervenes would conversation occur. This mutual seclusion, however, has been qualified in one important respect: for the good reason that none other has been available, the two styles of politics have shared a common vocabulary. They speak the same language and for the most part they theorize the same familiar institutions of government. But since each style of politics understands the words and

---

[4] 'Because you carry yourself as less than the gods, you command.' I fear that my sketch of the politics of scepticism may be confused with what has been called 'the nightwatchman state'. If possible this confusion should be avoided. I am not here considering 'the state'; I am considering only the activity of governing.

expressions of this common vocabulary in opposite senses, their communication has been for the most part at cross-purposes and the vocabulary has been confirmed in its ambiguity. That total misunderstanding has not ensued is due only to the fact that many of the words in this vocabulary have a range of meanings at the centre which to some extent mediates the extremes to one another.

When we come to consider some of the historic versions of these two styles of politics we shall be able to observe this ambiguity in action and, I hope, get a closer view of the concrete character of our politics, seeing it as a *concordia discors* of these two styles. But in the meanwhile I propose to offer two examples of the abstract manner of the ambiguity, in order to disclose the ease with which the vocabulary adapts itself to diverse uses.

There is a famous expression which comes to us from the ancient world: *salus populi suprema lex esto.* Thus it appears in Cicero.[5] And if it is an exaggeration to say that it has never gone out of currency since it was first written, it has certainly remained part of the stock of European political expressions ready to be drawn upon in times of need. In the succeeding centuries it has been quoted, misquoted, adapted, abridged and parodied. It has been in the service both of the politics of scepticism and of the politics of faith, and long ago it became a masterpiece of equivocation, the emblem of all the ambiguity of our political vocabulary. If the expression had been designed for ambiguity, it could scarcely have been better designed; every word in it is potentially double-tongued except the last, and that was usually omitted.

Let us begin with *salus.* Its meaning, even in classical Latin, ranges widely: from mere *safety* (relief from threatened extinction), through *health* (which is normal), and *prosperity* (which is modest), and *abundance* (which is excessive), and *welfare* (which is comprehensive), and on *salvation* (which leaves nothing to be desired). *Salus* in the Roman political religion was a deity of many parts, a goddess who personified at once health, prosperity, and public welfare.[6] And in Roman ears the expression *salus populi* must unavoidably have suggested the *salus publica* or *Romana* which was the care and gift of this goddess. And yet in this passage Cicero gives it a much narrower meaning; indeed,

---

[5] *Leg.*, 3. 3. 8.
[6] Cicero, *Leg.*, 2. 11. 28; Tacitus, *Agricola*, 12. 23.

the context is military. When the enemy is at the walls, when the very existence of the *civitas* is in danger, in those circumstances the first consideration of the general commanding the army is to be the *salus* of the *populus Romanus*. Prosperity, happiness, the good life – these have receded; their place is taken by the urgency of mere survival. The word *salus*, then, begins its political life in the service of the politics of scepticism, the politics of preservation, and moreover at the extreme. And in its original form, or translated into modern European languages, it has remained available in that sense. Committees of 'public safety' are not set up in quiet times when men's minds turn to thoughts of prosperity and well-being, they belong to times of emergency; their office is not to distribute abundance, but to counter famine, not to promote health but to deal with a plague, not to dispense welfare but to rescue from extinction.

No doubt the place *salus* came to occupy in the vocabulary of the Christian religion, meaning salvation from sin and its penalties, encouraged the exploration in politics of some of its wider meanings. The Middle Ages seem to have had little use for this phrase of Cicero; but when we meet it first in modern English politics it is as the formula of the royal prerogative, that 'mass of powers, rights and immunities which distinguished the king from a private individual' and which, in the sixteenth century, was beginning to be understood as the royal discretionary power not contained in the sum of statute and common law and exerted outside Parliament. This prerogative, no doubt, is the authority to set things right which have gone astray in an emergency. But it is not only this. And in appropriating *salus populi* as its formula, what was meant was (something wider than 'public safety') the 'general benefit of the realm'.[7] The word here, then, has already risen, but not very much, in the scale of its potential meanings. But it was not long before the expression was winging its way beyond this middle distance. Bacon, characteristically, after reminding judges that their office is *jusdicere* and not *jus dare*, advises them also to be guided by the maxim *salus populi suprema lex*, which, if they had listened to the advice, would have turned their courts into the sort of tribunals we have become familiar with – 'people's courts', judging not crimes but undefined misbehaviours, and dispensing not justice according

[7] cp. Chief Baron Fleming in Bates's Case (1606) Prothero: *Statutes and Constitutional Documents* (1558–1625), p. 341.

to known law, but some other sort of 'justice', 'social justice' perhaps. And when those who had abolished the monarch and his prerogative came to consider the regulative principle of government, its 'fundamental law', they more often than not chose this Ciceronian tag. It was given a great diversity of interpretation, appearing as the formula for radical antinomianism and as the formula of a strict constitutionalism, and the meaning of *salus* was enlarged: it meant 'the public good', 'the public welfare', 'the prosperity of the nation', and these in turn were interpreted as 'the establishment of true religion', the 'rule of righteousness' and the 'salvation' this signifies or in some more modest manner. It is not, then, remarkable that the sardonic Selden should find that 'there is not anything in the World more abased than this Sentence, *salus populi suprema lex esto*'.[8]

Nor was *salus* the only ambiguous word in the expression. *Populus* with the Romans was the equivalent of *civitas* or *respublica*. Cicero always uses *salus*, usually meaning 'security' or 'safety' in the narrow sense, in relation to the *civitas*.[9] And it is clear that those who took this expression as the formula of the prerogative read *populi* as 'realm'. And others coming after held to this interpretation. But there were those for whom *populi* acquired an exclusive meaning, not *populus*, but *plebs*; and thus emerged the vulgar contemporary meaning of 'the people'. Some even read the maxim as if *populi* referred to each individual subject; indeed, Locke, with typical inadvertence, does this on more than one occasion. *Suprema* displayed a similar ambiguity: sometimes it meant 'fundamental', at others 'overriding'; it stood for what was to be considered in the first instance and what was to be considered in the last resort when all other guides are silent. Nobody. I think, interpreted *lex* as 'statute' in the proper sense; the *salus populi* was regarded as the dictate of the *lex naturalis* but it was often written about as if *lex* were *jus*.

When Latin gave place to English as our political language, the range of meaning and the ambiguity of *salus* was inherited by the words which came to replace it, the words 'salvation' and 'security'. Pitt said that England had 'saved' Europe by her example and herself by her exertions, and it is clear that he was speaking from the bottom of the range of the meaning. He

---

[8] *Table Talk*, CIII.
[9] *Rep.*, 1. 1. 1; 1. 34. 51; 2. 23. 43; 6. 12. 12. *Ver,* 2. 2. 6   16; 2. 1. 2   4.

meant 'saved' from being 'conquered', 'rescued' from an oppressor. And if the revolutionaries would have translated this into 'saved' from being 'liberated', 'rescued' from being 'saved', the rise in meaning would be significant but mediated in such a manner as not to make it unintelligible. But when a politician in opposition today says to his constituents, 'When the General Election comes, you must turn out the present government, for then, and then only, shall we have a chance to save mankind,' we are aware of having taken flight to another world. And what is true of the word 'save' is equally true of the word 'security'; indeed its range of meaning and its ambiguity is too notorious to require illustration.

My second example concerns the word 'Right'; and here the situation does not need much elaboration. The word 'right' when preceded by the indefinite article enjoys a scale of meanings which ranges from one extreme to another, the extremes of meaning being, I contend, the meanings respectively appropriate to our two styles of politics. At the bottom end of this scale, 'a right' denotes the authority to enjoy certain treatment at the hands of others or to conduct oneself in a certain manner, these being joined with a method of seeking redress or compensation for any frustration that may be suffered. And, generally speaking, it will I think be found with 'rights' at this end of the scale that the means of redress has come first and the 'right' has been subsequently formulated as an inference; and usually the formulation is a little more liberal than the means of redress is able to secure. Thus, we normally have a right not to be imprisoned for more than a short period of time without a trial being set on foot, and a right to go free if after trial we are not convicted and if no further charge is preferred against us. And, in general, a writ of habeas corpus is our means of redress. Again, with certain exceptions, I have a right not to be refused entrance to a British university on account of my religious beliefs; which means that I can bring an action against those who do refuse me on those grounds; which, in turn, means that if they do not want me they must think of some other reason for refusing me. My right is, really, the right not to be given this reason for being excluded. Further, I have a right not to be arrested by a policeman unless he has reasonable ground for believing that I have committed a felony and if I am so arrested I can bring an action against the policeman. And again, I have a certain liberty of speech, and if I want to know precisely what it is, I can only find out by considering what freedom of speaking I have which will not make me liable to be proceeded against. In other words, my right is somebody else's duty and the right and the duty mutually define one another.

Now, some of the rights that have been proclaimed seem rather larger than those we have been considering; the rights, for example, to 'life, liberty and the pursuit of happiness'. And with these the meaning of the word 'right' begins to expand. For long enough we have been accustomed to reassure ourselves about this expansion by means of adjectives; we recognize the rights at the lower end of the scale as 'legal' rights, and we go on to denote others as 'moral' or 'social' rights. But this strategem solves no riddles. What is significant about the rights at the bottom end of the scale is not that they are 'legal', but that they are narrow; and what is significant about the rights which appear as we go up the scale of meaning is not that they are 'social' or 'moral' as distinct from 'legal', but that they are large; some of them indeed as we shall see are 'legal'. Now, what is the 'right to life'? Is it the right not to have my life extinguished except by due process of law? Or is it the right to enjoy a certain sort or standard of life? If it is the first, then we are still at the bottom end of the scale; if it is the second, then we have begun to move in the direction of the other extreme, though we may still be talking about a 'legal' right. Life, in short, is an ambiguous word, and 'the right to life' reveals the potential ambiguity of the word 'right'. And what is true of 'life' is true also of 'liberty' and 'the pursuit of happiness', except that here (but not everywhere) the last is more guarded; it stops short of proclaiming the right to obtain happiness. And so we may go on up the scale and perhaps we may regard ourselves as having reached the top when we come to the right proclaimed in another famous declaration, the right to 'freedom from want'; though there is no reason for it to feel lonely at the top – there are plenty of others of the same kind. But if this is a 'right' (and it might be a legal right, although it would require definition), then it certainly is not a 'right' in the same sense as freedom from arbitrary arrest is a 'right'. We understand easily what Scaliger meant when he said that in France 'everyone has the right to write, but few have the ability': but we have slid into a different world when we claim the ability to write as a 'right'. And what has become of the word in the famous saying of the Revolution: 'every Frenchman has the right to meet the enemies of his country in the field'?

Here, then, is the same range of meaning as we observed in the case of *salus* as a political word. At one end of the scale I may have the duty of preventing the weeds which grow on my land from corrupting my neighbour's land and be actionable if I fail in this duty; at the other end I may be given the duty as a farmer of cultivating my land 'according to the rules of good husbandry' and a legal penalty may likewise be attached to failure. At one end of the scale there is the right not to be arrested arbitrarily; in the middle, perhaps, is 'welfare', the right of the pregnant woman to have orange juice at the general expense of the community; and at the other end there is the proclaimed right to freedom from want. At the bottom, or near the bottom, is the *droit de travail*; in the middle (or perhaps rather further up than the middle) lies the *droit au travail*; at the top is the 'labour camp'.

Now, the extremes of meaning have corresponded, it seems to me, with what is respectively appropriate to the politics of scepticism and the politics of faith. Indeed, I have elicited these two styles of politics from the extremes of conduct and understanding which reveal themselves in our manner of speaking, and they are cogent formulations only in so far as they make intelligible the current and historic distraction of our politics. The ambiguity, of course, springs simply from the employment of a single word for diverse and opposed conceptions.

So far, then, we have before us the abstract designs of these two manners of governing and two manners of understanding what is proper to the office of government. And we have observed also what may be called the mechanism of the ambiguity. Our next task will be to consider the fortunes of the politics of faith and the politics of scepticism.

3

THE FORTUNES OF FAITH

I

The general character of the politics of faith is before us; we must now consider the emergence of this style of politics in modern times, and consider some of the versions in which it has appeared.

In the politics of faith, the activity of governing is understood to be in the service of human perfection; perfection itself is understood to be a mundane condition of human circumstances; and the achievement of perfection is understood to depend upon human effort. The office of government is to direct the activities of its subjects, either so that they contribute to the improvements which in turn converge upon perfection, or (in another version) so that they conform to the pattern imposed. And since this office can be sustained only by a minute and zealous control of human activities, the first need of government in the politics of faith is power to match its task.

It would seem, then, that anyone seized of the principles of this style of politics would be active first in accumulating the power necessary to make a start on the enterprise. This, or something like it, may very well be what happened; but not, I think, at the beginning. Abstract, speculative ideas about the office of government, or about anything else, do not spring up spontaneously in this manner; and as a general rule I think it will be found that what men wish to do has its roots in what they can imagine themselves doing with the abilities and resources they already command or plausibly hope to command. At any rate, the thesis I wish to investigate is that, in the modern history of Europe, the politics of faith is not the parent of a great increase in the quantity of power at the disposal of government, but a child of a circumstantial enlargement of that power. The appearance, not suddenly but in a remarkably short space of time, of greatly increased quantities of power, some of it already annexed to the office of government and all of it potentially at the disposal of government, and the promise of almost limitless additions to that power – these happenings, which mark the emergence of the modern world out of what we call the Middle Ages, beckoned the practice of government in the direction of an ever more minute control of the activities of the subject and themselves generated the beliefs which belong to the politics of faith. In other words, my contention is that the power which began to be acquired by European governments in the early years of our period was not required in order to pursue a style of government supremely in need of great quantities of power, but that this style of government emerged when the requisite power to conduct it had appeared, and it did not recommend itself in the abstract either to the ruler or to the subject until long after it had in some degree established itself. It is *not*, however, my contention that this accumulation of power was the necessary and sufficient cause of the appearance of the politics of faith: history knows no such necessary and sufficient causes. I suggest only that, in the modern world, the politics of faith was one of the offspring of this circumstantial accumulation of power. I shall argue later that the other notable offspring (perhaps by a different mother) is the modern politics of scepticism. Or perhaps it would be a more accurate account of my view to say that both these styles of politics are the step-children of that enlargement of power which marks the beginning of modern times.

Now, this thesis might, I think, be defended on general grounds. It might, on the other hand, be established historically – that is, by showing in detail the emergence of this understanding of government and of the power conditions of early modern history. I shall pursue neither of these causes: not the first, because while I might convince myself I doubt if I should convince anyone else; and not the second, because my knowledge is insufficient. I shall make no attempt to prove my thesis: instead I shall do my best to make it convincing by exploring it as a plausible hypothesis and by observing what it reveals.

In the politics of faith, the office of government is to direct and integrate all the activities of its subjects; ideally no movement is made which is not inspired or at least approved by the governing authority. This may come about in either of two general circumstances. It may happen in a community in which governing as a separate and limited activity has never appeared because such distinctions as those between private and public, or between religious and secular affairs have never been recognized. Or it may happen in a community from which these and other similar distinctions have been eliminated by the extension of the competence of government to an all-embracing activity. There is, then, what, if some latitude is allowed, may be called a primitive version of the politics of faith. The minute control characteristic of a primitive community is possible only because such communities are small and compact, because their activities are limited in variety and relatively untouched by the impulse to improve, and because the distinctions which would qualify overall control are either inchoate or have never been made. The power to operate this style of 'government' is sufficient because in these conditions it does not need to be very great. Of course, in default of adequate power to persevere in this style of politics, the activities of the subjects will tend (as we know from modern times) to be reduced to what can be controlled, and the notion of perfection will be approximated to a condition which seems to be within the power of government plausibly to provide or to be about to provide. But such reduction is not called for in a primitive community: there power to control and the activities to be controlled are not discrepant because they have been born and bred together.

In the conditions of modern Europe, however, the situation is different. The immense power characteristic of modern governments was notoriously lacking in the governments of the preceding age. I do not mean merely that, owing to lack of power in government, public order in the Middle Ages was often to seek, that (as Macaulay says) 'an insurrection was got up then almost as easily as a petition is got up now'. This may be true, though its significance is qualified by the fact that even public order by no means depended for its maintenance upon the power vested in the prince. I mean that there was altogether lacking the power and resources necessary to operate that minuteness of control which is characteristic of the politics of faith. The distinctions had long ago been made between religious and secular affairs (though in practice they were distinctions difficult to observe), and though the notion of 'public' was weak, that of 'private' was less weak, and the idea of the centralized direction and integration of the activities of the subject was far beyond the horizon. My contention is, then, that it was neither virtue nor vice, neither wisdom nor stupidity which kept our medieval ancestors from the politics of faith; it was merely the manifest incompetence of governments to pursue this style of politics which stood in the way of the enterprise ever entering their heads. And the immense but gradual change which above everything else marks the emergence of modern out of medieval Europe was the appearance of governments with enough power and resources to make this style of politics seem a possibility and to inspire it.

During the late fifteenth and sixteenth centuries, governments all over Europe were, in varying degrees, acquiring a power to control the activities and destinies of their subjects such as their predecessors had never enjoyed; power, indeed, in excess of that enjoyed by any government hitherto, except the 'governments' (scarcely distinguished as such) of far smaller and far less diversified communities. This increase of power was generated by countless small changes, each hardly significant in itself, which may be seen to fall under two general heads. It represented, first, a collection under the hand of the monarch and his associates in government of all the powers of control and integration which had hitherto been exercised, with varying degrees of independence, by a great number of different authorities, some of them personal and specific and others impersonal and customary. And secondly it represented the participation of government in a share of that great increase of technical ability to control men and things which was characteristic of the time.

The process of assembling at one centre hitherto widely diffused powers of government has long been recognized (but not always properly interpreted) as one of the most important of those modifications of medieval life and thought which constitute the emergence of modern from medieval Europe. In various degrees, and at differing rates of progress, it took place all over Europe, but nowhere more rapidly or more conclusively than in England, where there was less to stand in its way. The desuetude of competing powers, the break-up of the hierarchical social order which had formerly been the main force of integration, the political mastery of the church, the development of a local administration under the hand and direction of the King's Council and its subsidiaries, and (what is emblematic of the whole change) the emergence unmistakably of a 'public' authority with a special status of its own – on account of all these things, before the end of the sixteenth century there had already come into being a sole central power wielding the totality of the authority commonly understood to belong to government. It was a totality greatly increased by the mere process of its assembly – a monopoly here, as everywhere, itself adding a quantum of its own to the powers it embraced. All this has been recognized by historians as the source of a great enhancement of public order in these political communities, and on account of this it recommended itself to the subject – particularly to the rising class of small landowner and merchant. If it brought autocracy nearer, that, within limits, was a price they were prepared to pay for that hitherto scarce commodity, order. And again, it has been recognized that it was this concentration of power in the control of government which made possible the success of all the successful political revolutions of later days, none of which has ever modified the pattern of government first beginning to be traced in the early sixteenth century and many of which have considerably elaborated it.[1] But what is significant for us is not the enhancement of public order, but the manner in which it made possible (and indeed inspired) minute government. For here was a government which was not only single and undisputed, but one which could with varying effectiveness enter into and control a vastly greater number of the activities of the subject than had hitherto been controllable by any power. The tireless, inquisitive, roving hand of government was beginning to be able to reach everywhere, accustoming the subject to the notion that nothing should be beyond its grasp, and opening up to speculative writers the vista of a future of limitless possibility. And from this point of view, much the most significant of all these changes was, I think, the gradual disappearance of the intermediate authorities which had formerly stood between a then weak central government and the subjects, leaving them naked before a power which in its magnitude was becoming comparable to a force of nature. This isolation of the subject, like so much else at that time, was not the design of a government already intent

---

[1] It was a failure to appreciate this which led to the misinterpretation in which the Tudor monarchy was represented as a hiatus in English constitutional history, and the misinterpretation of French history which represented the French Revolution as a break-away from the practices of the seventeenth-century French monarchy. Both these errors spring from an exclusive attention to the authorization of government and the neglect of the activity of governing.

upon minuteness; it was a displacement, a circumstantial change which made such government possible. Many times since the sixteenth century, new intermediaries between the lonely subject and his government have been set up, but the politics of faith has always recognized them as inappropriate to its purposes, and in so far as this style of politics has prevailed, they have maintained themselves with difficulty or not at all. Partly by chance, then, and partly as the result of policy[2] (though never of very far-seeing policy), a government better equipped to conduct the politics of faith was emerging in the early years of the modern period.

Nor did the enlarged powers of government to control and integrate the activities of its subjects in early modern times spring only from this centralization of authority: they sprang also from the participation of government in the vast increase of the ability to control men and things which was at that time on foot; indeed, without this participation the centralizing process would have been abortive. For power is not an abstraction; it is the ability to act quickly, economically, with effect and with certainty; and this ability is not itself the offspring of centralization. Everything that adds to man's mastery over his world, everything that makes human effort and energy more productive and more economical, when appropriated to government (and there is little of this which is inapt to the activity of governing), makes the politics of faith more possible, and therefore (my contention is) more attractive.

At the time of which I speak, then, the power of government was also being enlarged by the application of more efficient techniques, most of which had already seen an apprenticeship in some other field of activity, in commerce or in industry. Indeed, almost the whole apparatus by means of which governments in our own day are able to exercise a minute control over the activities of their subjects – the apparatus of banking and book-keeping, the records, registers, files, passports, dossiers and indexes – was already waiting to be exploited. Without ease of movement and communication, without a ready supply of paper and ink, without all those reports and records which spring up whenever paper, ink and human curiosity are joined, without a settled common language, without a literate population, without

[2] One piece of policy, going back a long way, which in England made it easier to harness Parliament to the politics of faith was the demand of monarchs for representatives with full authority to speak for their localities.

ready means of identification, without settled frontiers, without (in short) a high degree of mastery over men and things, the prospects of the politics of faith are nugatory; with them, there is little to stand in their way.

All these things were already available to governments in the sixteenth century, or were only just over the horizon. Indeed, in this matter the only overwhelmingly important additions which have appeared in modern times have been the by-products of electricity: telegraphy (which enabled Abdul Hamid to massacre his Armenians with incomparable efficiency),[3] and the telephone, without which politics of faith would long ago have lost half their charm by losing most of their impetus. No doubt Philip II's administration of his empire was, by our standards, cumbersome and inefficient, but compared with what could have been done a century earlier, it was a marvel of inexorable minuteness. In short (my point is obvious) the conditions which make possible the politics of faith had already emerged in the sixteenth century in an amplitude so greatly in excess of what had before existed that it is scarcely an exaggeration to say that they had appeared for the first time.[4] The stage is set, the actors are assembled; it remains to enquire what piece is to be put on and whether the characters have learned their parts. Government displays a power of control compared with which all earlier displays are counterfeit; it remains to consider what modification in the understanding of the office of government the possession and exercise of this power induced.

The spectacle of government with so much power already at its disposal, together with the forecast of what might appear if it were to avail itself of all the improved techniques (as they come forward) of controlling and directing the activities of men and were itself to promote the improvement of such techniques, provoked a variety of responses. It was welcomed with enthusiastic applause as the dawn of an era of hitherto unheard-of happiness; and it was observed with apprehension. And in these

[3] Abd al-Hamid II (1842–1918). Ottoman sultan, 1876–1909. Known as the 'Great Assassin' for his role in the Armenian massacres of 1894–6.

[4] The writings of Fulke Greville, first Lord Brooke (1554–1628) are remarkable from many points of view, but not least because they reveal a man who is overwhelmingly impressed with the *power* at the disposal of government. He recognizes it as a 'restless', 'undertaking' power, but his attitude towards it is ambivalent: he is inspired by its potentialities for 'public good' and at the same time he is apprehensive of the disparity between human wisdom and the power invested in government.

opposed responses emerge the politics of faith and the politics of scepticism in their modern forms. We are concerned now with the response of optimism; and it is proper to consider this first, not because it was the most far-seeing, but because its voice was loudest and few were altogether unmoved by the energy of its utterance.[5]

The partizans of power, in those days, were many; and in their hands a new understanding of the office of government gradually took shape. They were all fascinated by the spectacle and the promise which revealed itself; and with varying degrees of insight (and with motives which ranged from a simple-hearted self-interest to a no less simple-hearted impulse to 'save' mankind) they explored and exploited what they recognized as the potentialities of their time. Indeed, there were so many of them that it would seem invidious to choose one as the emblem of this response. But as it happens, there was one who (so far as England was concerned) represented this attitude in so complete and unqualified a manner, and who (so far as Europe in general was to be concerned) did more to promote it than any other man, that we may safely turn to him as, in this respect, the mirror of his age and the chief architect of the politics of faith: Francis Bacon.

---

[5] There were, of course, other responses to the situation which concerned themselves with matters of detail. For example, the questions of the authorization of political power and of the grounds and limits of obedience to government both assume a vastly greater significance with every enlargement of the power of government. Who would not find these questions 'academic', questions to pass a night in discussing but which lost their cogency with the return of daylight activity, if the power exercised and the demands made were small and rarely felt? And even if, on occasion, the demands were great – if they included a demand to fill an emergency by risking one's life in defence of one's country – even this circumstance would not be nearly so effective in giving practical importance to these questions as lesser but more numerous and more nagging demands, demands felt every day and every hour of every day, demands such that even the privacy of one's bed afforded no escape from them. The gathering importance of these questions in modern times is a commentary on the energy of the politics of faith: would 'conscientious objection' have any relevance apart from this style of politics? These questions were preeminently important in the sixteenth century because the demands of government in respect of religion were inquisitive and minute; and they have remained important because, in so far as the politics of faith has been practised, the demands of government have grown ever more inquisitive and more minute in respect of all kinds of human activity.

There were, of course, many before Bacon who understood the activity of governing as the exercise of power: Machiavelli, for example. But none of the characteristic ideas of the politics of faith appear in Machiavelli's pages. He understands the activity of governing as the exercise of power for maintaining order and securing the continuance of a political community; there is no hint of a minute and brooding authority engaged in the tireless direction of all the activities of the subject, no hint (indeed, quite the reverse) of a mundane condition of human perfection to be promoted or imposed in this manner. He is a sceptic who understands the ruler, not as the patron of perfection, but as a defence against chaos and indeed against extinction. Machiavelli keeps studiously to the bottom end of the range of meanings which the European political vocabulary was beginning to offer. And moreover, it is to be doubted whether the political power with which he was familiar was great enough to suggest the possibility of the control and integration of all the activities of the subject. With Francis Bacon, however, we are in a different world: an immense vista of human improvement is opened up before us, and government (using and promoting the extension of every intimation of power to control and master men and things) is the chief agent in a pursuit of perfection. Indeed, there is no turn or twist in the subsequent history of the politics of faith (except some of its grosser exaggerations) which is not adumbrated in his writings.

The details are intricate, and must be passed over. The first principle of the politics of faith is the vision of human activity as the pursuit of human perfection, and the careful reader of Bacon's writings may doubt whether he can find in them anything so precise as this. Bacon, he may conclude, is concerned with improvement rather than perfection; but he may conclude also that Macaulay was going too far in saying that 'to make man perfect was no part of Bacon's plan. His humble aim was to make imperfect man more comfortable.' It is true (and it is appropriate to many versions of the politics of faith) that Bacon never leaves the impression that he expects a transformation of human character, but there is a mundane condition to be pursued or imposed which he regards not quite as the birth-right of mankind, but as the restoration of what the race lost at the Fall (though perhaps not on account of the Fall). This condition may now be achieved, if at all, by human effort; and it may be described as a condition in which mankind has the power to exploit and is fully exploiting, for their own benefit, all the resources of the world; a condition, that is, in which the race enjoys the maximum 'well-being' that the world allows. That the climax should ever be reached, that a new golden age should appear, Bacon scarcely considers; his mind runs more to the notion of an endless pursuit in which each stage has its rewards. But we cannot on this account absolve Bacon of 'perfectionism'; the road is chosen because of its exclusive excellence. It is not doing him an injustice, then, to recognize that this pursuit is regarded by Bacon as a redemption of mankind in history. His message was that when the whole weight of human effort is methodically organized to oppose it, the imperfection of man's condition will, in a large measure, disappear; and that this is the proper engagement of mankind. The late sixteenth century was asked to choose between two theories of the condition of the world; that things were getting worse and that things were getting better, that the world was old and spent and that it was young and vigorous; and to oppose the theory of progress was to enhance the theory of decay.[6] Bacon, temperamentally, was not disposed to indulge in speculative opinions, and he ranged himself with the optimists in this matter largely because he believed that the conditions of human life could be vastly improved by human effort and because he suspected (like Hakewill)[7] that a general theory of decay 'quails the hopes and blunts the edge of men's endeavours' and was likely to rob human effort of much of its energy and divert mankind from its proper business.[8]

It is, I think, wise not to pay great attention to Bacon's often expressed dissatisfaction with the way things were going in his day; he was not in fact born in 'le sein de la nuit la plus profonde', and it was pointed out to him at the time that he exaggerated the indifference and ignorance of his contemporaries. It is true that the staple occupations of mankind were still

[6] The choice was again presented in the early nineteenth-century in the writings of Chateaubriand, de Maistre and Bonald. We, fortunately, are required to make no such rationalistic choice; general decay and general progress are alike suspect.

[7] George Hakewill (1578–1649), author of *An Apologie or declaration of the power and Providence of God in the government of the world: Consisting of an examination and censure of the common errour touching natures perpetuall and universall decay* . . . , 1st edn 1627, 3rd revised edn 1635. An influential work opposing, as did Bacon, the view that nature and human beings must decay.

[8] Bacon, *Works* IV. p. 90.

governed by craftlore and folklore, but the intimations of change in this respect were visible to those who looked. Moreover, Bacon participated in that great tide of restless curiosity about the world which distinguished his time and which provided the energy he wished to canalize. But the twist he gave to learning was significant, though here also he was improving upon an unacknowledged inheritance. Briefly, it may be called a utilitarian, but not a narrowly utilitarian, twist. Knowledge, he perceived, could provide power, and the organized pursuit of knowledge would provide power rapidly and in great quantity: it was power he was interested in, and he imagined it as the mastery of the world for the benefit of mankind. Bacon, then, was inspired by the possibility of vast accessions to knowledge accompanied by a corresponding enlargement of mastery. And what he communicated to his own and later generations was, first, an excitement at this prospect; secondly, a faith that it was not out of reach on account of any radical defect in human nature; thirdly, a confidence that diligence would be rewarded; and fourthly, a method (or at least the outline of a method) by which it should be pursued: the valuable characteristics of this method were its certainty and its ease. Indeed, later generations derived from Bacon an almost magic certainty, not only that knowledge would accrue and power follow, but also that they had at last been put on the road proper for human beings to tread. Effort, of course, was necessary, but the yoke was easy and the burden light. And if there is genuine modesty (as there is) in Bacon's hopes for mankind, there is also a supremely confident Pelagianism: a faith in the redemption of mankind in history and by human effort.

But joined with this there is something else. Bacon was inspired by the capacity he saw in mankind to achieve its own 'well-being'; indeed it may be supposed that his belief that the pursuit of 'well-being' is the exclusively excellent activity for mankind sprang from the correspondence he observed between human capacity and the achievement of 'well-being'. But he was inspired also by the power he observed to be already at the disposal of government. And he makes no secret of his conviction that the office of government is to be the chief patron of perfection and the *primum mobile* in this enterprise of mundane salvation. 'Well-being' itself is power, mastery over the resources of the world; but its pursuit also requires power, mastery over human activity to set it on this course and to keep it there with the maximum economy of human effort. On any reading, great power would be needed to direct this enterprise; but even greater power is required when 'perfection' is understood (as Bacon understood it) as a perpetually pursued mastery of the resources of the world which is never complete, than when it is imagined (as in the conventional utopia) as a settled condition for the imposition of which only a fixed amount of power would be necessary, although this amount might not at first be easy to estimate. Government, therefore, in virtue of its power is to direct the enterprise of salvation; and in virtue of this office more power, indeed unlimited power, must be given it.

Bacon did not overlook some of the circumstantial difficulties of this position, but he speaks with confidence. The governing authority (authorized rather by its power and intention of conferring 'well-being' rather than by any more formal authorization, such as divine right or popular consent) appears in his writings as almost external to the society, regulating it from the outside; and governing is the minute control of all the activities of the subject – a control designed to convert these activities of the subject into the pursuit of 'well-being'. It is the art of 'settling the condition of the world'. Its business is to supervise industry and trade, to improve agriculture, to eradicate idleness and waste, to regulate prices and consumption, to distribute wealth, to endow learning, to settle religion (so that it should not interfere with the enterprise of mundane salvation), and, of course, to preserve order and guard against a foreign foe – all, in fact, and a little more than all that was already present or intimated in Elizabethan government. Bacon had a native prudence; just as he deprecated the over-early and peremptory formulation of general scientific theories, so in government (the pursuit of 'well-being') he advocated cautious experiment before any great new project was undertaken, but that government should lead mankind in the recovery of 'that right over nature which belongs to it by divine bequest' he had no doubt at all. He is rarely arrogant in his writings, and it is not to be expected that no relics of a more sceptical style of politics should sometimes appear. Nevertheless, they impart a certainty that at least the direction in which he points is right and that there is no reasonable alternative. He displays also in detail many of the subsidiary characteristics of the politics of faith: an absence of scruple, a suspicion that formality in government and an insistence on the letter of the law will hinder the enterprise, a dislike of amateur meddling in government, a preference for prevention over punishment, no abhorrence of retrospective legislation, and a predominant interest in the future.

In short (and this is the only inference I wish to draw at present), the writings of Francis Bacon afford evidence that, even before the end of the sixteenth century, government had acquired the necessary power for the pursuit of the politics of faith and had in fact set out on this road, and that the principles of this style of politics were beginning to be understood: both the style and the understanding of the style had unmistakably emerged. Minute government, where the power exists, may be undertaken and defended for a variety of reasons. What I have called the politics of faith is present only when minute government is understood in terms of the pursuit of 'perfection', and this is how it is understood in the writings of Francis Bacon.

II

The politics of faith (this enterprise of the minute direction by government of all the activities of the subject in the service of perfection, where 'perfection' is understood, not as a type of human character, but as a mundane condition of human circumstances) is clearly capable of a certain internal variety: there is usually more than one idiom of 'perfection' offering itself for pursuit. Indeed, there are potentially as many versions of the politics of faith as there are interpretations of the meaning of 'perfection'.

The character and extent of the control exercised will, of course, be relative to the power available, but (unless special hindrances intervene) they may be expected to be always as minute and as wide as power permits. A government in this style which is not always at the end of its tether would be a psychological and moral enormity: to economize in power would be to economize in perfection, an activity indistinguishable from folly. But further, the power available must also be expected to be at least one of the conditions determining the perfection pursued. Indeed, it may happen that 'perfection' comes to be defined by the kind and extent of the power available almost to the exclusion of any other consideration. And when this is so, men, by a simple process of self-deception, convince themselves, not that they 'ought' because they 'must', (a pardonable aberration), but that they 'ought' because they 'can'.[9] But usually the kind of perfection pursued is determined by a wider context than mere consideration of power: habit, a long indulged direction of attention or some specially alluring promise, to say nothing of smaller or more temporary provocations, enter in to determine the character of the 'perfection' to be pursued.

In modern times the politics of faith has exploited two main idioms: there has been a religious version, and there has been what may be called, in a general way, an economic version. In the religious version the powers of government are employed (and, of course, are understood to be properly employed) in imposing upon the subject a pattern of activity so absolute and exclusive as to leave no room for things indifferent, which is taken to be 'perfect' in the sense of being righteous. What I mean by the economic version, which is itself susceptible to a certain internal variety is, generally speaking, that of which we have already seen Francis Bacon to be the prophet.

Now, the first thing to be observed about the religious version of this enterprise is that it is intelligible only in the context of modern history. Sometimes it is assumed to be a peculiarly medieval idea and to have survived into the modern world because civil authority in the sixteenth century took over, along with its other acquisitions, powers which had earlier been exercised by the Church. But this, I think, is a misunderstanding. Civil authority, it is true, appropriated powers which had earlier belonged to ecclesiastical offices or courts, but if anything is unmistakably foreign to medieval ways of thinking (to say nothing of being vastly in excess of the power available anywhere in the Middle Ages) it is the notion of government, lay or ecclesias-

---

[9] This is the obverse of what Locke (a man not given to cynical observation) remarked upon. 'It is worthy to be observed and lamented that the most violent of these defenders of the truth, the opposers of errors, the exclaimers against schism, do hardly ever let loose this thin zeal for God, with which they are so warmed and inflamed, unless where they have the civil magistrate on their side. But so soon as our court favour has given them the better end of the staff, and they begin to feel themselves the stronger, then presently peace and charity are to be laid aside. Otherwise they are religiously to be observed. Where they have not the power to carry on persecution and to become masters, there they desire to live upon fair terms, and preach up toleration. When they are not strengthened by the civil power, then they can bear most patiently and unmovedly the contagion of idolatory, superstition, and heresy in their neighbourhood of which on other occasions the interests of religion makes them extremely apprehensive.' *A Letter Concerning Toleration* (Gough), p. 134.

tical, imposing a single pattern of activity which is believed to be righteous upon the subject. Indeed, such a pattern appears in Europe only when traditional manners of behaviour and traditional diversities of calling and activity are neglected, or are put on one side, in favour of a model of conduct believed to have been found in the Bible. Of course there is medieval teaching about how men should behave in all sorts of circumstances, but there was no single comprehensive model of righteous conduct which it was thought government should enforce, and aberrations from the accepted model were punished, even by the Church, not as detestable errors but as dissidence dangerous to order.[10] In short, this religious version of the politics of faith is intelligible only in a world which has been modified by Protestantism.

Seventeenth-century Europe provided many examples of this version of the politics of faith, and among the most revealing are those to be found in the history of English puritan politics. It is my contention that every historic situation in modern politics, every significant concrete political movement, cause or party, contains within it particles of both the current styles of politics. It is perhaps possible, but even that is rare, to find a person wedded exclusively to one or the other, but as a rule where faith is a wife, scepticism is a mistress; and the lover of scepticism will be found also to be the friend of faith. For, as I have suggested, these styles are tendencies towards extremes, the extremes themselves alone being genuinely exclusive of one another and rarely embraced. It is not to be expected, then, that so comprehensive a movement as the politics of English puritanism should display an exclusive allegiance to either of these styles, or that such allegiance as it does show to one or other of them should be confined to a single idiom. Nevertheless, the clearest examples I know of the religious version of the politics of faith appear in the history of puritan politics: it appears unmistakably in the politics of the Presbyterian party and in the politics of the various millenarian sects.

The politics of English puritanism appeared first as the politics of opposition; and what was opposed was the current government and in particular its ecclesiastical settlement. This could be

---

[10] Acton, 'The Protestant Theory of Persecution' in *The History of Freedom* ed. and Intro. by J. N. Figgis and Laurence Vere (London: Macmillan, 1907), pp. 150–87.

opposed from either of two points of view: because any general settlement which imposed a uniform system was objected to; or because a uniform system was desired, but not this one because it is identified as error. The first is the opposition of scepticism, and among the puritans was represented by Brownists, Congregationalists and Independents. The second is the opposition of faith, and is represented by the Presbyterians who wished to impose not only an ecclesiastical settlement of their own, which they believed to be in favour of 'true' religion, but also to impose by government a single comprehensive pattern of activity upon all subjects without exception, a pattern which they identified with righteous conduct. That is to say, they opposed all other religious beliefs than their own, not because a variety of religious belief was observed to be liable to provoke disorder,[11] but because all but their own were identified with 'error'. The constitutional question, the question of the authorization of government, was, of course, secondary – merely a means to the end of establishing an omnicompetent government wedded to the pursuit of righteousness.

The Fifth Monarchy men and the other millenarian sects display the religious version of the politics of faith in an extreme form. For these, the activity of governing was precisely the activity of grace imposing itself upon nature to bring about a condition of things identified as 'Salvation'. It is a mundane condition of things, and except perhaps where it was connected with a belief in the imminent Second Coming of Christ, it does not escape the 'Pelagianism' characteristic of the Baconian enterprise and all other versions of the politics of faith in the modern world. The aim of these men was to establish by government a 'holy community' in which the only significant distinction was between the saints (who were to rule) and the unregenerate (who were to be ruled). Moreover, this project was not a distant utopia, remote from the circumstances of the time. It sprang, as I believe all versions of the politics of faith spring, from a vision of power: it seemed to these men that God had providentially put into the hands of the Parliamentary army the necessary power to inaugurate the reign of righteousness. And, as was to be expected, they displayed all the consequential dispositions of those who embrace the politics of faith: formality in government gives place to activism governed only by the posses-

---

[11] This was the contention and point of view of Hobbes.

sion of power and the zeal for righteousness; no scruple is permitted to stand in the way of imposing the pattern of perfection; prevention is preferred to punishment; and no power is deemed too great to harness to the pursuit of righteousness.

There were, of course, other parties among the puritans who looked in the direction of faith, just as there were parties and persons who stood for a sceptical style of politics, and many who, like Cromwell and Ireton, show the impress of both styles. But what is interesting, and what leads us on from the religious version of the politics of faith to what I have called the economic version, is that even the most unmistakable appearances of the religious version were qualified by the intrusion of the economic version, which itself rapidly came to supersede all others in the modern world. This alliance between the two interpretations of 'perfection' in puritan politics may be traced in detail; the great puritan writers, to say nothing of the less articulate rank and file, are indelibly Baconian. But this will appear paradoxical only to those who forget the large common ground occupied by all versions of the politics of faith: the particular idiom is always less significant than the common understanding of governing as the activity of imposing a mundane condition of things designated as 'perfection'.

In what I have called the economic version of the politics of faith, the powers of government are employed (and are understood to be properly employed) in directing and integrating all the activities of the subject so that they converge in the pursuit of a condition of human circumstance denoted by such expressions as 'well-being' or 'prosperity' and represented as the kind of 'perfection' proper to be sought by mankind. But here we must be discriminating. The practice of all European governments in the seventeenth century was to impose, by regulations of varying minuteness, a pattern upon all the activities of the subject: in one degree or another all European communities were regulated communities, and the regulator was the central government and its servants. This regulation, the offspring of power and utterly unlike anything the Middle Ages has to show, normally extended as far as power permitted; and in what may be called, generally, the economic sphere, it is named mercantilism by historians. It was, of course, the counterpart of the religious uniformity imposed or attempted by most of these governments. But mercantilism may be interpreted as a version of the politics of faith only if it is understood as government imposing a condition of human circumstance because it is regarded as 'perfect' or productive of 'perfection'. And this was certainly not always the case in the seventeenth century. The practices of mercantilism, or many of them, may be, and in fact often were, understood not as the integration of activity for the purpose of achieving a 'perfect' or even an improved way of living, but (for example) merely as unavoidable elements in a policy determined by considerations of national defence: they were even recognized as costs in the balance sheet of 'well-being'. And when they are understood in this manner (related to a limited enterprise and therefore themselves subject to a limit) they belong, of course, to the politics of scepticism and not of faith: they are no part of an intention of 'establishing heaven upon earth'.[12] But there is no doubt also that, even in the early seventeenth century, they were coming to be understood as the appropriate practices of a government which had the power and the duty of organizing all the activities of the subject in order to establish a condition of things desired on account of its 'perfection'. And, of course, this is the understanding of them that appears in the writings of Francis Bacon. In this version of the politics of faith, then, the pattern of activity to be imposed may be called 'productivist': government is the organization and direction of a 'productivist' society.

The 'productivist' version of the politics of faith emerges first in the sixteenth century. It was nurtured by many circumstances, and exhibits the characteristics of all the current ambitions, and all the current moral values, and not least the contemporary admiration of diligence, suspicion of leisure and horror of idleness. Early in its career forecasts were being made, not only of the conditions it would involve and the power it would require, but also of the benefits which would accrue from the pursuit of this enterprise – that is, forecasts of the detailed character of the condition of human life to be established.[13] But from our point of view, what is significant is not the benefits to be enjoyed (the detail of the 'perfection'), but the belief that this enterprise of the maximum exploitation of the resources of the world is one into which all human activity should be integrated and therefore an activity proper to be inspired or controlled by the only

---

[12] This, for example, is the understanding of Bodin and Mun.

[13] Apart from the various utopias of the seventeenth century, of which Bacon's *New Atlantis* and Burton's sketch in the preface to the *Anatomy of Melancholy* are good examples, there were more matter-of-fact forecasts, such as E. Chamberlagne, *England's Wants* (1667).

authority which has the necessary power of overall direction, namely, government. For it is this belief, the faith that a 'productivist' community is the only community in which human perfection can be achieved (and not merely the pursuit, among other things, of a higher standard of living) which constitutes a version of the politics of faith. And this belief expresses itself in the extended (as opposed to the narrow) meanings of the words in our political vocabulary. 'Security' becomes first 'welfare' and then 'salvation', 'work' becomes first a right and then a duty; 'treason' is recognized as unfaithfulness to a moral or a religious creed; and every minimum is converted into a maximum until 'freedom from want' and the enjoyment of happiness, are proclaimed as 'rights'. Just as Beza considered it the business of government to suppress religious dissent, not as a danger to order but as *error*, so the productivist considers it the duty of government to suppress as *error* all opposition to his enterprise.

Now, although the general outline of the pattern of activity to be imposed upon the subject in this style of politics was early perceived and embarked upon without waste of time, the details (both of the kind of activity it would require from government and the kind of benefits to be enjoyed by the subject) emerged slowly. And in the fortunes of this style of politics there is no more important a chapter than that which recounts the elaboration of this enterprise in the writings of its eighteenth-century protagonists – the *philosophes*.

This notable collection of writers, which included many of the leading intellects of the day in all European countries, are sometimes represented as the originators of the theories which sustain this version of the politics of faith. But in fact the part they played was to formulate, in a manner appropriate to the intellectual climate of their age, all the practices and projects which their predecessors in this style of politics had painfully hammered out. In their writings, what had remained obscure became clear, what was hitherto tentative became certain, what was emergent emerged. The materials upon which they worked were not only the writings of their predecessors (and here Francis Bacon and Locke were preeminent), but also the practices of government which had been elaborated during the seventeenth century: the techniques of oversight and control which had already endowed governments with extraordinary power. In France, as the precursors of a revolution which was to give the name of 'freedom' to a style of government hitherto thought of as slavery, nothing of their inheritance was lost to them. Where Bacon had deplored a contemporary darkness, these luxuriated in a contemporary enlightenment. And elsewhere it was the same: in destroying the old superstitions they formulated the new. And what, among much else, they bequeathed to their successors was a clear understanding of the exploitation of the resources of the world as the proper activity of mankind and of this activity directed and integrated by government: a sublime confidence in the exclusive propriety of a 'productivist' manner of living. They occupy, of course, a place in the history of our ideas about the composition and authorization of government, but that place is of little importance compared with their contribution to the elucidation of the politics of faith. For this style of governing is not essentially connected with any particular constitution or with any particular ideas about the authorization of government. There may be some constitutions which are specially susceptible to its charms and others which seem naturally to turn away from it; but, generally speaking, these apparent affinities and repulsions are insignificant.

The later fortunes of the politics of faith, in the nineteenth and twentieth centuries, are intricate and eventful. They reveal examples of this manner of government more splendid than any that had hitherto appeared. Vast new sources of power were opened up and exploited. And the extension of the characteristic benefits which spring from the style of politics has, with many, removed any lingering uncertainty they may have suffered about the exploitation of the resources of the world as the exclusively proper activity of mankind. Four centuries of enjoyment and self-deception have at last moralized the productivist enterprise. The great wars of our age have given us an unrivalled opportunity to carry out expensive experiments in this style of politics, and it is perhaps only the cost which keeps us from the final assault on the heavenly city. On the other hand, we have to observe with regret that the significance of power is always in relation to its task, and while power to integrate has increased so has the variety of human activities to be integrated. The skill of the bowler is greater, but so also is the versatility of the batsman; and perhaps, after all, the net situation, in this respect, is not so very different from what it was in the early seventeenth century – or would be if the technique of reducing activities to those which can be integrated had not in recent times advanced so rapidly.

But with all these new adventures, the elucidation and defence of this style of politics remains where the great protagonists of the eighteenth century left it. The tactics have vastly improved, and the defenders of faith have found it possible to dispense with a few outdated eccentricities. But in the grand strategy no new principle of any intellectual significance has appeared, although several have presented themselves for our consideration. A few novel phrases have been added – 'social engineering', 'planning for plenty' – but their idiom is still unmistakably Baconian. And after four and a half centuries of meditation the conclusion still is that 'our consideration of human nature in relation to welfare . . . has shown that man has the possibility of almost complete control of his fate, and that if he fails it will be by the ignorance and folly of men':[14] which is, after all, no more than what Bacon himself said.

III

Now, I have done nothing more than to recall in briefest outline a passage in the history of modern politics. But of the many conclusions to which this history directs us, three I think are preeminently important.

First, the politics of faith are not the invention of the last hundred and fifty years as a reaction against a period of governmental indifference and negligence. They are not either a wise or a futile response to contemporary or near-contemporary difficulties. They are a style of politics, pursued in more than one idiom, which is coeval with the modern world, and its emergence is one of the modifications of medieval life and thought which constitute the modern world. To abridge its history is to mistake its character, and to make it seem much less significant than it is. The growing preoccupation of government with 'the management of the life of the people' which the Macmillan Report of 1931 identifies as 'a change of outlook of the government of this country in recent times' is, in fact, a style and understanding of government which has been with us for five centuries. And it is now to be counted as irrepressible as any other.[15] To regard it as

[14] E. L. Thorndike, *Human Nature and the Social Order* (1940), p. 957.

[15] The Macmillan Committee was established in 1929. Hugh Pattison Macmillan presided over a distinguished committee of economists including J. M. Keynes (the principal writer of the report), Bevin and others to

the folly or the wisdom of a few eccentrics or seers, as the product of the French or of the Industrial Revolution, or as the faithful consort of something called 'democracy', is altogether to misunderstand it.

Secondly, it is not to be identified with any concrete political movement, party or cause in the modern world. There have been representatives of this style of politics in every camp, every party, every movement and among the advocates of every cause. No doubt there are some movements which seem to embrace it almost to the exclusion of everything else, and this is certainly the case with what we know of as socialism and communism. But in fact no concrete political movement of any significant dimensions in the modern world has, in this respect, escaped complexity. The politics of faith are not, and never have been, the exclusive property of any European country or any political party. This style of politics is merely one of the two poles between which all modern political enterprise and understanding have swung for five centuries.

Thirdly, the politics of faith are not, and never have been, the only, or the only significant, style and understanding of politics which the history of the modern world discloses. Some writers, and among them some of the most influential, have been so impressed by the glory or the enormity of this style of politics that it fills the whole field of their attention: for them the course of modern politics, and particularly its course during the last hundred and fifty years, is nothing else but the story of the fortunes of this style. Some make this mistake out of despair: the cloud of faith seems to them to have hung over us for so long that it fills the whole sky and darkens the whole earth. Others make it out of optimism: to see the history of modern politics as the gradual triumph of what they believe to be good adds pleasure to approval and delight to confidence. With others, again, it is not a mistake at all, but a piece of dissimulation: to suppress everything in the history of modern politics but the fortunes of the politics of faith is a preliminary to suppressing everything but this style of politics in the contemporary world. 'We know the direction in which the world is moving and we must bow to it or perish': such is the counterfeit predicament these writers put upon us. But although the infection springs from diverse sources, the prophylactic is the same in each case.

discover whether arrangements for banking and finance, both internal and international, enhanced or restricted trade and industrial employment.

It consists in a more thorough and a more candid study of the history of modern politics. For this will at once reveal strains in our politics other than that of faith and will dispose of this mistaken or disingenuous theory of a single direction. Even the most ignorant historian knows that the one certain way of misreading the course of events is to select some feature in the past and to read the course of events as if it converged upon that one goal: a single experiment in this manner will demonstrate conclusively how much of what actually happened has to be wantonly dismissed from the story in order to achieve this result. And clearly a no less misleading abridgement appears when the course of events is read as if it converged upon some feature of the contemporary world (for example, the present popularity of the politics of faith) selected as its one goal. In short, we do not know 'the direction in which the world is moving', not because we lack evidence which might reveal that direction, but because the notion of such a direction depends upon a distinction between legitimate and illegitimate offspring which is foreign to historical study. A single, homogeneous line of development is to be found in history only if history is made a dummy upon which to practise the skill of a ventriloquist.

4

THE FORTUNES OF SCEPTICISM

I

The politics of faith, as I have described them, are a creature of modern times. Their versions have been various, but all of them presuppose the circumstances which in respect of government distinguish modern from other times. The religious version, for example, which we are tempted to regard almost as an anachronism in the modern world, is, in fact, such that it could not have appeared (for example) in the Middle Ages; and while it seems to have some sort of affinity to the political style of an ancient Greek city state, it is an affinity which ceases to be convincing as soon as we leave generality for concrete detail. We have, it is true, observed that a primitive society, where the relations and activities of its members are controlled with a minuteness which even the vast power of a modern government has never been able to equal, exhibits something that may perhaps be recognized as a counterpart to the modern politics of faith. But it is never more than a shadowy counterpart: strictly speaking these communities have no politics, and in place of what we know as 'government' there is only the unspecialized care and guardianship of their general interests by those of its members who have charge of the administration of their customs.

In the same manner, the politics of scepticism, properly speaking, have the conditions of the modern world as their context, not because they exist only in opposition to the politics of faith, but because they presuppose the same conditions as those which make possible the politics of faith. Nevertheless, if for a moment we confine ourselves to generalities, the modern politics of scepticism may be recognized to have counterparts elsewhere. They are, generally speaking, the politics of the powerless, the style and habit of governing appropriate to circumstances in which government enjoys only a small opportunity of directing the activities of its subjects. And in these circumstances they are likely to be the accepted style of understanding of politics. Small extensions of power, limited enlargements of activity, may be imagined and, being imagined, may be sought as desirable; but nobody thinks it negligent or improper for a government not to be doing what, with the power it actually enjoys (or some small extension of it), it cannot even be imagined to be doing. Consequently, it is not far-fetched to recognize in the government of medieval England, for example, a counterpart to what in the modern world emerges as the politics of scepticism. Indeed, as we shall see, the tactics of this style and the principles of this understanding of government in the modern world are greatly in debt to medieval practice and reflection.

And again, the government of a conqueror will naturally gravitate in the first place towards the sceptical style: the subjects, because they resent it doing anything, will think (if they think at all) that it ought to do little; and the conqueror, in the best of circumstances, will be able to do only little. The conqueror today, it may be thought, is able to impose a comprehensive pattern of activity on his conquered subjects in a manner unknown in earlier times: what neither the Roman nor the Turk attempted is now the common enterprise in conquest, and the conquered subject has come to expect it, even to welcome it, as his fate. But even the contemporary conqueror is often obliged to modify his ambitions, and in the early stages the sceptical enterprise of 'pacification' will take precedence over everything else and will determine his style of governing. And further, in a community where, on account of defeat in war or some natural calamity such as the spread of plague or famine, superficial order is threatened or disrupted, the sceptical style and understanding of government will be recognized as appropriate. In short, in any conditions where the power at the disposal of government is liable to be exhausted in maintaining the superficial order of the community, the politics of scepticism will be the accepted style and understanding of government.

A style of politics, however, exists only in its versions; and while the observation of these generalities may be a suitable beginning to an investigation of the politics of scepticism, their concrete character appears only when we turn to consider them in the conditions of modern times. And, of course, the outstanding feature of these conditions is the appearance of governments with a reserve of power beyond what appears to be necessary for the maintenance of superficial order. In the modern world the context of political scepticism is the presence, not the absence, of power.

II

But before we begin to explore the territory which this observation opens up, there is one aspect of the politics of scepticism which may be disposed of first because, although it has a place in the fortunes of the style, it is a relatively unimportant place. I mean the politics of scepticism merely as a reaction against the politics of faith.

We have already noticed the error involved in regarding the history of modern politics as merely the unfolding and eventual flowering of the politics of faith. In this misconceived success story, scepticism, of course, appears among the forces of darkness and is identified with 'reaction'. But if we put this on one side as partizan history, it nevertheless remains true that each of the major triumphs of faith in the modern world has provoked a movement in the opposite direction. Indeed, my thesis, that the history of modern European politics is an unsteady wavering between these extremes, anticipates the appearance of a pull in the opposite direction whenever the practice and understanding of government swings near to either of its theoretic extremes; and it forecasts that each of our styles will in turn become 'reactionary' as it sinks out of fashion or begins once more to capture the initiative. And the plausibility of regarding scepticism as the mere opponent of faith lies in the historic situation in early modern history when the tide was set in the direction of the politics of faith, and scepticism appears, for this important moment, as an impediment. As the story unfolds itself, this situation is, of course, in general, repeated at intervals.

It belongs, then, to the fortunes of scepticism to appear as the opponent of faith, and on these occasions it takes its shape and colouring from the immediate situation. An early example of an occasion of this sort is provided in the history of the English Civil War. We have seen that the civil commotions of seventeenth-century England, though they were not by any means a simple struggle between faith and scepticism, threw up parties which embraced a religio-economic version of the politics of faith and understood governing as the activity of imposing a comprehensive pattern of activity upon the community, a condition of things which was identified with 'salvation'. And some who took this view regarded the victorious Parliamentary army as the providential means for establishing 'righteousness' and the 'rule of the saints'. If this pressure upon English politics to take the direction of faith, and follow it to the extreme, had been the work of a few eccentrics, it could be expected to subside without having to be opposed. But it had behind it not only significant power, but also what was becoming a well-articulated body of ideas and arguments, both religious and secular, and consequently it provoked opposition. And the extremity of its enterprise is attested by the fact that many of its opponents, like Cromwell himself, were politicians who in other circumstances were more likely to find themselves in the camp of faith than that of scepticism.

These sceptics, Cromwell, Ireton, the Levellers of the *Agreement of the People* and others, can be seen springing back from the vista of the politics of faith, the door which they had helped to open, very much as some socialists today spring back from a vision they have helped to propagate. The arguments of Cromwell and Ireton in the Putney Debates,[1] the early proposals of the Levellers and the arguments of the Independents were an exposition of the politics of scepticism which took its shape and colour from the particular version of the politics of faith that it was designed to oppose. The activity of governing is represented, not as the establishment of abstractly 'good things' or a 'perfect' condition of human life, but as conditioned by what 'the nation are prepared to receive and go along with' – Cromwell had 'few extravagant thoughts of obtaining great things from Parliament'. A crude and elementary philosophy of 'expediency' is appealed to; the antinomianism of Buffcoat and Wildman is opposed by a sceptical doctrine of formalism and of the binding force of even inconvenient engagements.[2] Governing appears,

---

[1] Debates in 1647 among members of the New Model Army about the meaning of their cause and the goals for which they were fighting Charles I.

[2] Buffcoat: actually Robert Everard, agent of Cromwell's regiment, a religious enthusiast who participated in the Putney Debates in 1647. Sir John Wildman (1621–93) was a Leveller who instigated resistance to Cromwell's negotiations with Charles I and who maintained that he 'could serve no man's will, and wished the liberty and happiness of his country and all mankind'.

not as 'settling the condition of the world' or promoting an undefined *salus populi* by the readiest means, but as the activity, limited by 'fundamental law', of protecting established rights; and even the element of contingency and conventionality in the 'fundamental law' is recognized. Political discussion is represented, not as the occasion of divinely inspired pronouncements, or even as the means of arriving at 'truth', but as an effort to understand diverse points of view and reach a *modus vivendi*.

Now, if we are inclined to regard this as a trifling incident in the history of the relations of faith and scepticism, the seventeenth and eighteenth centuries, both in England and on the continent, provide an example of an encounter between these two styles of politics which, though it may easily be misunderstood, is not inconsiderable; namely, the sceptical opposition to the economic version of the politics of faith. Nevertheless, its dimensions may be exaggerated if we do not observe the proper distinctions. Mercantilism, as we have seen, the enterprise of a national economy regulated in more or less detail by government, does not essentialy belong to the politics of faith; indeed, it is amenable to a sceptical explanation and defence, and it belongs to faith only when it is understood in the Baconian manner as part of a comprehensive plan to direct all the activity of the subject to the exploitation of the resources of the world in the belief that this is the activity preeminently proper to mankind. The minute and inquisitive regulations of Colbertism, and the similar enterprise of English governments, both Royalist and Parliamentarian, in the seventeenth century were, therefore, criticized from two different points of view.

First, there were those who opposed them because they believed them to be inefficient. So far from promoting the 'prosperity' which was taken to be the proper pursuit and destiny of mankind, they believed them to be a hindrance: in the way of the most economical exploitation of the resources of the world. This opposition clearly falls short of what I have called scepticism. It is true that there is doubt here about the competence of government to promote plenty, but the fundamental assumption of this version of the politics of faith, that an acquisitive society is the appropriate home for a human being, is accepted without misgiving. The objection is not to the enterprise of exploitation but only to the manner in which it is being conducted.[3] But secondly, there were others who were relatively indifferent to the efficiency or inefficiency with which this activity of government promoted a productivist society: they objected to imposition of a productivist pattern upon the society because they objected to the imposition of any comprehensive pattern of activity; they opposed this version of the politics of faith because they would oppose any version. And it is these who bring to bear a genuinely sceptical criticism. Indeed, it is to be assumed that their objection to this version would have been even stronger than it in fact was if this method of promoting the 'Pelagian' state had showed signs of being more efficient than it appeared to be: its inefficiency was almost a merit, intimating as it did that success was to be judged by other criteria. To this school belonged a distinguished body of writers; to go no further than the great names, Hume, Burke, Bentham, Macaulay, and, I think, Adam Smith himself, the context of whose opposition to this version of the politics of faith was not merely an *ad hoc* doubt, but a profound understanding of the principles of political scepticism. And, when their attention is directed to this version of the politics of faith (which was not always the case), the objection of this school of writers was not merely to its lack of economy: they detected in it a whole miscellany of errors – its overoptimistic reading of human behaviour, its tendency to

---

[3] There were, of course, many cross-currents of opinion within this school of critics. The clearest statement of the point of view is to be found in the works of disinterested writers, of whom there is a long line beginning in the early seventeenth century. And here the reader may be referred, for example, to Lipson, *Economic History of England*, vol. III. But it would be a mistake to assume that this was the point of view of every industrialist and merchant eager to make a fortune on his own account. These, it is true, were often accused of neglecting the 'common prosperity' for their own profit, and their accusers often based themselves on the disingenuous view that communal acquisitiveness is somehow morally superior to individual, a view always favoured by the partizans of power. In the main, what the merchants objected to were specific regulations, and they left to others the task of stating the general objections. And this is what we shall expect. It is within our own experience that it is exceptional for a business community not to take the line of least resistance in respect of the regulations of government, regarding them merely as additions to the normal costs and hazards of trade. Such a community will look for (and usually find) means of reducing the hindrance to a minimum, and will even discover ways of turning the imposed conditions to its advantage. The businessman is, normally, a critic of the politics of faith only at two removes.

impoverish mankind by reducing all activity to that which could easily be controlled by government, its radical misconception of the political significance of private property, its bringing the law into disrepute by requiring it to attempt what it could not accomplish, and its promotion, at home and abroad, of that insecurity which in their view it should be the chief office of government to mitigate.

III

But to understand the politics of scepticism merely as opposed to the politics of faith is to understand them imperfectly. Scepticism did not spring up merely as a reaction to faith; it sprang up, in the modern world, in response to the circumstances which made possible the politics of faith. And the resources it drew upon were provided both by some of the circumstances of the modern world and by what may be called, if some latitude is allowed, its inheritance from the medieval understanding of the office and operation of government.

The immense enlargement of the power of man to control human activity was the context of the fond optimism that has been abroad in Europe since the sixteenth century and which, in some measure, has replaced Christianity by a version of Pelagianism. The participation of government in a large share of this power was the condition of the appearance of the politics of faith. It would seem, then, that political scepticism would be without any standing ground in the dawn of modern history: opposed to the contemporary tide, its only generation would seem to be from an abstract idea, the notion, merely, that what was afoot was undesirable. And to extract in detail a sceptical style and understanding of politics out of this idea would seem to be the contemporary task of those who believed it. But in fact the scene at the beginning of modern history is by no means filled with the ambitions and enterprises of faith: not only were there among the circumstantial changes taking place in the office and operation of government some which favoured scepticism, but in addition there was a native tradition of scepticism uninspired by any opposition to the certainties of faith, and there were also lively relics of a sceptical attitude in politics inherited from the past.

Alongside the enlargement of political power (which inspired the politics of faith), there went a greater definition and specification of the office of government. Government in the early modern period was beginning to appear as a 'public office' with a special status (soon to be spoken of as 'sovereignty') distinguishing it from the agglomeration of authorities which were understood to belong to the monarch as a person, because they were in effect only intensified private rights. The mediation of this appearance is recorded not only in the history of the legal status of government and its servants, but also (for example) in the history of the 'prerogative' in England, and in the history of taxation and public finance which records the conversion of what had hitherto been a royal income into a national exchequer. This change was a more narrow specification of the activity of governing, and it provoked the view that to govern was not the exercise of an undefined guardianship over the activities of the subject, but the performance of certain public duties. In short, while the enlargement of power pulled in the direction of faith, the concomitant narrowing in the specification of government pulled in the direction of a sceptical style and understanding of politics: closer definition of office evoked a limitation of the sphere of activity.

But besides this circumstantial aid to scepticism in politics, the style in the early modern period drew upon a native diffidence in respect of human power which survived, not without some difficulty, the dazzling prospect of the Baconian enterprise. We are apt to regard the strain of doubt and despondency which appears in so much of Elizabethan and early seventeenth-century literature as a relic of medieval pessimism not yet regenerated by the optimism of Bacon and his associates, or as a wanton, faithless hesitation to take the tide at its flood: in fact, it was neither, but an alternative view of the powers and prospects of the race which faith has never been strong enough to obliterate. This disturbed vision of the weakness and wickedness of mankind and the transitoriness of human achievement, sometimes profoundly felt (as in Donne and Herbert), sometimes philosophically elaborated (as in Hobbes, Spinoza and Pascal), sometimes mild and ironical (as in Montaigne and Burton), was, when it turned to contemplate the activity of governing, the spring of a political scepticism independent of the suspicion which the triumphs no less than the projects of faith might be expected to generate. It has been said, often enough to merit contradiction, that what divides scepticism from faith in politics is a belief in the doctrine of 'original sin'; but this is too hasty a generalization. Not only were the puritan protagonists of the politics of faith (Milton, for example, among them) as firmly convinced of the truth and significance of this doctrine as anyone else, but Bacon himself does not doubt it; and both Hobbes and Spinoza (whose understanding of politics was preeminently sceptical) were profound, if oblique, critics of the doctrine. It is not a belief in 'original sin', but something much nearer home and less abstract and speculative which distinguishes the sceptical politician in the early modern period: a sense of mortality, that *amicitia rerum mortalium*, which detracts from the allure of the gilded future foreseen in the vision of faith; the earth recognized not as a world to be exploited but as a 'player's stage'; and a doubt in respect of the turn-out of human projects, especially when they are largely designed, which suggested that mankind should at least pause for reflection before committing itself to a single line of movement. It is, then, a very foreshortened view of the late sixteenth and early seventeenth centuries in which they appear as an age of confidence and faith; and we need only turn to Bacon's great contemporary, Michel de Montaigne to find a sceptical comparison to the forward-looking enthusiasts of the time, so convinced that they are on the right road.

Montaigne has no illusions about human power. Custom in human life is sovereign; it is a second Nature, and no less powerful. And this, so far from being deplorable, is indispensable. For man is so composed of contrarieties that, if he is to enjoy any coherence of activity or any tranquility among his fellows, he requires the support of a rule to be obeyed. But the virtue of a rule is not that it is 'just', but that it is settled. Indeed, even by common standards, customs as they exist and laws as they are administered are more likely to be 'unjust', and they are certainly never more than contingent and municipal: we obey them because they serve their turn, and nothing more imposing than this can be claimed for them. And as for the enterprise of making the arrangements of a society subserve human perfection, or of imposing a comprehensive pattern of activity upon the subject, it is a project out of touch with the conditions of human life. *Que sais-je*: what am I so certain about that I would direct all the energy and activity of mankind to attaining it? And to sacrifice the modest orderliness of a society for the sake of moral unity or 'truth' (religious or secular) is to sacrifice what all need for a chimera. Montaigne could have corrected from his own experience the errors of those optimistic historians who have suggested that at this time governments had so far established peace and 'security' that it was proper for them to go forward with the enterprise of organizing 'prosperity'.

But the politics of scepticism at this time, particularly in England, had additional resources to draw upon, an inheritance that spoke directly in habit and institution and needed no elaborate interpretation in order to divulge an understanding of government in this style. The characteristic of medieval government was not only its relatively small power, but also a comformable notion of governing. The great institutions which it bequeathed to the modern world were all of them courts of law of various kinds, and the understanding of government which they carried with them was that of a *judicial* activity. And on any reading of its office and competence, a court of law is not the kind of institution which is appropriate to take the initiative in organizing the perfection of mankind: where governing is understood as the judicial provision of remedies for wrongs suffered, a sceptical style of politics obtrudes.

This is illustrated most revealingly in the history and character of the English Parliament.[4] It is clear that the Parliament of the thirteenth and fourteenth centuries was not only understood to be a court of law, but was in large measure modelled upon the courts which already existed and to which it was reckoned to be superior. The representatives who were called to Westminster were recognized as suitors to a court in the same manner as a freeholder in the county and the hundred was an obligatory suitor to his county and hundred courts. And just as the task of the suitors in the inferior courts was to 'find' the law and to 'ascertain' the custom, so it was understood to be the task of the suitors at Westminster, in consultation with the King's justices (who as late as the beginning of the fifteenth century seem to have been regarded as an 'estate' of Parliament), to 'find' the law in the wider and more authoritative context of the kingdom. The practices of the early thirteenth century show 'a direct line of connection between the county courts and the King's Council, already established and in frequent use'.[5]

That the Westminster Parliament was understood as a court set over other courts for resolving difficult or doubtful

[4] See C. H. McIlwain, *The High Court of Parliament*, and G. L. Haskins, *The Growth of English Representative Government* (from which I have drawn most of my information).

[5] G. B. Adams, *The Origin of the English Constitution*, p. 321.

judgments and providing new remedies for newly emergent wrongs and meting out justice to all according to their deserts[6] is clear, not only from the writs which called the representatives together (which required experts in the law), and from what contemporaries wrote about the nascent institution, but also from the procedure followed at its meeting. To hear petitions for the redress of grievances was among its most ancient tasks. Indeed it is clear that what was later to be recognized as 'legislation' sprang from a small and almost imperceptible enlargement of the exercise of a judicial office; and the taxes which it early became customary to vote were first understood as no more than the revenue of the King's High Court of Parliament, 'profits of justice' in principle indistinguishable from the 'fines' of the King's Bench.[7] It may, perhaps, be argued that in this early period we have a condition of things in which the distinction between judicial, legislative and administrative activity has not yet been recognized; and there is truth in this contention. But what is significant is that the character of judicial activity is well recognized and understood and that 'legislation' and 'administration' are understood in the judicial idiom.

All this is common knowledge about the character of medieval parliaments, and it is relevant here because even in the seventeenth century, Parliament is still understood as a court of law. A contemporary of Bacon writes of Parliament as 'the highest and most authentical court in England';[8] and in the middle of the next century the Commons are referred to as 'the greatest and wisest inquest in England'.[9] Moreover, whatever enlargements were taking place in the business handled in Parliament, the early centuries of the modern period had constant and explicit experience of its working as a court of law in which trials were conducted and judgment pronounced. 'It required time, a long time, and great changes in the State . . . to alter all this and subordinate the old idea of a court to the newer one of a legislature.'[10] And the slowness of the change is one of the measures of the relative weakness of the politics of faith (to which 'legislation' is indispensable) and the relative strength of the politics of

---

[6] Haskins, *The Growth of English Representative Government*, p. 6.

[7] Ibid., p. 111.

[8] Sir Thomas Smith, *De Republica Anglorum* (ed. Alstan), p. 58.

[9] *Fitzharris's Case* (1681), see C. Grant Robertson, *Select Cases and Documents*, p. 420.

[10] McIlwain, *The High Court of Parliament*, p. 121.

scepticism.[11] For, as I have said, where governing is recognized as the activity of a court, the office of government will be understood as the maintenance of 'rights'[12] and the redress of 'wrongs' and not as the imposition of a comprehensive pattern of activity upon all the subjects of the realm. In short, in the early centuries of the modern period, the best-established interpretation of one of the most significant of English political institutions was an interpretation in the sceptical idiom.

IV

The sceptical style and understanding of government was, then, by no means without a firm foundation, especially in England, in early modern history. And in the years that followed it not only found a number of exponents of its principles, but it also adapted itself in a series of versions to the changing circumstances of the modern period. It is, often, to be found in express opposition to the politics of faith and it was never without a current answer (cogent or otherwise) to the current versions of faith. But in the main the pattern it took was not determined by the twists and turns of the politics of faith. It developed by exploring more deeply the intimations of its own complex world of ideas, by coming to understand itself more fully in the circumstances of the modern world and by drawing upon the resources of the wider tradition of moral scepticism fed by such thinkers as Bayle, Fontenelle and Shaftesbury and Hume, which extends from the sixteenth century to our own day. On occasion it can be seen to be following a blind-alley; but it never lacks vitality, and

[11] The opinion may be ventured that the strength which enabled the English Parliament to survive the eclipse which overtook representative institutions on the continent in the early modern period (when the activity of governing was everywhere coming to be understood in the idiom of faith) sprang in some measure from the recognition of its judicial character. Assemblies which were not at all or not preeminently judicial, such as the States General of France, succumbed, while judicial assemblies, like the Parlement of Paris, survived. It must always be more difficult for a government, however powerful, to abolish what is understood as a court of law than an assembly which lacks this character.

[12] The 'rights' and 'duties' themselves, of course, were not recognized as 'natural' or primordial; they were known to have been established by a judicial process out of the 'tangle of personal relationships' which preceded their formulation. F. M. Stenton, *The First Century of English Feudalism*, p. 44; Haskins, *The Growth of English Representative Government*, p. 25.

its triumphs, though perhaps less spectacular (on paper) than those of faith, were usually more solid, and were triumphs not only in reflection but also in political invention. Two of the three great revolutions of modern times began in the style of scepticism; and while the first issued in the most profoundly sceptical constitution of the modern world, the Constitution of the United States of America, the second, the French Revolution, was soon diverted into the path of faith.[13] The Russian Revolution alone owed nothing to the politics of scepticism. Moreover this understanding of politics provided a characteristic interpretation or a characteristic criticism of all the new political devices and arrangements, manners of behaviour and institutions which began to proliferate from the beginning of the nineteenth century.

It has been my contention that the politics of the modern world are the *concordia discors* of these two styles of government, and consequently we shall not expect to find any writer or party wedded to one to the complete exclusion of the other. But it is not difficult to discern writers who lean heavily in the direction of scepticism, and to distinguish these from others who lean towards faith, and others again who exhibit the *concordia discors* itself in their often muddled thought, of whom the most important is John Locke. Among the more notable political writers, at the level of principle, who propounded versions, often very individual versions, of the politics of scepticism are Spinoza, Pascal, Hobbes, Hume, Montesquieu, Burke, Paine, Bentham, Hegel, Coleridge, Calhoun and Macaulay. This may be thought an ill-assorted gallery, and so from other points of view it is. But in whatever respects they diverge from one another (and often the divergence will be found to be on the question of the authorization and constitution of governments) they have in common a rejection of the political 'Pelagianism' which lies at the root of all modern versions of the politics of faith, a rejection of the belief that governing is the imposition of a comprehensive pattern of activity upon a community and a consequent suspicion of government invested with overwhelming power, and a recognition of the contingency of every political arrangement and the unavoidable arbitrariness of most. England has been peculiarly

---

[13] The Declaration de Droits de l'Homme et du Citoyen of 1789 is a sceptical document and is often in the pattern of the English Declaration of Rights of 1689. The version of 1793 has already begun to be infected with the politics of faith.

the home of this understanding of government; and in English political literature there are examples of a revealing kind of writing in support of this style of politics which are not easily to be found elsewhere – writing which touches, but lightly, upon principle but which is alive in every line with the idiom of scepticism. I am thinking particularly of the writings of Halifax and Burke, and at a lower level of the authors of the *Federalist.*

The earliest triumph of the politics of scepticism was the recognition of the distinction between politics and religion. This distinction was, of course, implicit in early Christianity, and it had been theorized with profound insight by St Augustine. But circumstances made it necessary to reestablish it both in theory and practice in the modern world, where the politics of faith had removed the boundary. Nevertheless, although even the seventeenth century has something to show in respect of a restoration of the distinction, the achievement then naturally had its immediate relation to the local circumstances of the time: the main enterprise of scepticism was merely to lend its weight to the view that it is inappropriate to saddle government with the task of determining religious 'truth', and in this manner to promote the view that if government were to establish and enforce any form of belief or worship it must be not on account of its 'truth' but on account of the disorder and insecurity which appeared to spring from the absence of an established religion. The immediate task of political scepticism was, at that time, to remove religious 'enthusiasm' from politics; and it was not until much later that the condition was ripe for a more radical attack on the problem. And indeed it gradually became apparent that this was not a problem which could ever be finally solved. The politics of faith is, from one point of view, the continuous reassertion of the unity of politics and religion; and from this point of view it is the comprehensive task of scepticism perpetually to be recalling political activity from the frontier of religion, to be always drawing attention to the values of civil order and *tranquillitas* whenever the vision of a total pattern of activity, imposed because it is believed to represent 'truth' or 'justice', threatens to obliterate everything else. And although the problem as it appears in *Hudibras,* or two centuries later in Macaulay's essay on Gladstone's *The State in its Relations with the Church,* is simple and direct compared with the problems set to political scepticism by more recent approximations of politics and religion, the problem itself is single and continuous.

In England during some part of the eighteenth century the

political style of scepticism may be said, for that moment, both to have won a great victory and to have revealed itself for the first time in modern dress.[14] It was the achievement of Whig politicians and of writers such as Halifax, Hume and Burke to have modernized its political devices and restated its principles in a manner appropriate to the times. What had hitherto remained an inheritance from the Middle Ages became a style and understanding of political activity practised and expressed in a modern idiom. Here again it is interesting to note that this style was not, or not for long, the exclusive property of any political party: for a time, the tide of political activity in England was turned in the direction of scepticism. And perhaps the greatest achievement of this period was to elaborate the practices and principles of a modern sceptical manner of diplomacy and the conduct of relations with other states – a manner which had no place for foreign policy as the prosecution of a religious crusade. But like the achievements of faith, this predominance of the sceptical style was not an interlude, but a moment in our political history from which it was recalled by a resurgence of faith. But before it passed, the principles of political scepticism had been reconstructed in a manner appropriate to the time.

But rather than the occasional triumphs of scepticism, what reveals the character of this style of politics more fully is its failures; not its periodic displacement by the politics of faith, but the occasions when it has behaved out of character. The chief of these, in modern times, was its *mésalliance* with the politics of Natural Rights and with the politics of republicanism.

It was, perhaps, unavoidable that a style of governing in which the office of government is understood as the maintenance of appropriate order, the preservation of rights and duties and the redress of wrongs should be ambitious to establish itself on a firm foundation. The impulse to assure ourselves that our arrangements and authorized manners of behaviour represent not merely fact and habit, but 'justice' and 'truth', and that they have a 'certainty' which is out of reach of the vicissitudes of time and place, has always been strong. But it is an impulse which belongs properly to faith. Historically, so far as scepticism is concerned, it must be regarded as an infection caught from faith, a temporary desertion of its own character induced by the plausible triumphs of faith. And that such a foundation should

---

[14] See H. Butterfield, *The Englishman and his History*, Part II.

be sought in the notion that the rights and duties to be protected are 'natural' and to be defended on account of their naturalness was an enterprise given in the climate of seventeenth-century opinion. The writer who led Europe in this respect was John Locke, the most ambiguous of all political writers of modern times; a political sceptic who inadvertently imposed the idiom of faith upon the sceptical understanding of government. But how out of character this enterprise was soon became apparent. To turn 'rights' and 'duties' which were known as historic achievements, elicited by patient and judicial inquest from the manner in which men were accustomed to behave, into 'natural' rights and duties was to deny them just that contingency of character which was the heart of the sceptical interpretation, and was to attribute to them an absoluteness and a permanence which in the sceptical understanding of them they could not possess. And political scepticism was recalled from its unnatural alliance with the politics of Natural Rights, not by the criticism of Bentham (which was never quite critical enough), but by the genius of Burke and Hegel.

Of all the follies of the politics of scepticism, the strangest is that which appears in the history of modern republicanism. There have been those, like Algernon Sydney, whose attachment to republicanism was one of adoration, who recognized it as the New Jerusalem and enquired no further. And again there have been republicans who believed that this manner of constituting a government was the only or the best means of making sure that the comprehensive pattern of activity to be imposed by government was after their liking and unmodified by extraneous or sectional interests: for them republicanism represented a government which could be trusted with unlimited power because in such hands this power would infallibly be used for the 'common good'.[15] This is republicanism interpreted in the idiom of faith.

But historically the more significant interpretation has been that of scepticism. The sceptical republican (and the best example of a writer of this persuasion is Tom Paine) saw in this manner of constituting government the infallible means of limiting the activity of government, of making government less costly, of diverting it from the enterprises of faith and concentrating its attention upon the necessary task of maintaining

[15] cp. Lamartine, *La France parlementaire*, II, p. 109.

peace and order – in short, for setting up a government fixed irrevocably in the sceptical style. Republicanism here is embraced because it is believed to be the one form of government in which the exercise of power will never be in the service of the perfection of mankind. And a modification of this belief is the root of the sceptical faith in the simple device of universal suffrage and popular government as an infallible specific against an over-mighty governing power, which appears in the writings of Bentham and James Mill. But in the fortunes of sceptical politics this alliance with republicanism is a surrender to visions and impulses which properly belong to faith.

The belief that there is a particular manner of authorizing and constituting government which will infallibly result in one and only one manner of exercising the power of government (and that a desirable one) is an illusion appropriate to the politics of faith, and that political sceptics like Paine and Richard Price (and to some extent Milton before them) came to entertain it reveals how insecure a grasp they had upon the principles of political scepticism. For the belief that immense power in the hands of government is innocuous so long as the government has been constituted in a certain manner could only be entertained by men who had forgotten the reading of human behaviour which makes political scepticism intelligible. The insistence of these writers upon annual parliaments (though as a device of limitation it was both impracticable and almost certainly ineffective) may be taken as a sign that they had not entirely forgotten their scepticism. But it is only in recent years, and under the pressure of contemporary experiences, that sceptical politics has begun to divest itself of this inconsistency.

V

In comparison with those of faith, the fortunes of scepticism are difficult to trace. The politics of faith have followed, often slavishly, in the wake of every enlargement of power (fortuitous or otherwise) which government in modern times has been given the opportunity of enjoying. And an account of their fortunes is in the main an account of the projects promoted in carrying out the grand design: the tactics have changed in the course of time, but the understanding of government has suffered no significant development in the last couple of centuries. The fortunes of the sceptical style, on the other hand, are not the story of projects undertaken, and are only to a small extent the story of political inventiveness: they are, more properly, the story of the perpetual reformulation of an understanding of government in order to keep it relevant to current circumstances. Scepticism has not always been successful in maintaining this relevance, and there have been times when the manifest pull in the direction of faith has kept it on the defensive, and times also when a sudden enlargement of power (not at all embarrassing to faith) has caught it on the wrong foot. But for the most part it has understood its task as that of keeping alive and relevant the magnetism of this pole of our political activity. As a rule, it has enjoyed a higher degree of self-discipline and self-knowledge than the politics of faith, and has rarely fallen to representing itself as more significant than it is.

In the last hundred years its greatest achievement has been intellectual: to strip itself of that faith in simple expedients which often in the past has qualified its character and restricted its usefulness. And of this there is no better example than what has happened to the doctrine of the separation of the powers of government which for so long was one of its chief expedients. At one time the separation of powers was regarded as a mechanical device in which specific activities involved in governing were to be kept in separate hands, with a consequent dispersal of the total power exercised by government. As a practical principle for the limitation of power, it never corresponded to the political structure of any community. And as a mechanical device it was never clearly intimated even in English political behaviour, and never became operative even in those constitutional constructions which were invented largely under its inspiration. It is not, then, to be wondered at that in the last hundred and fifty years it, too, lost rather than gained in significance. It was soon swept aside as a mere hindrance to the enterprises of faith; and where faith has gone farthest, even the most cherished item in this construction, the independence of the judiciary, has been involved in the collapse. But instead of merely discarding it as a device too antiquated for use in modern circumstances, political scepticism has succeeded in eliciting from this over-formal doctrine a more profound principle and a reading of politics preeminently relevant to contemporary conditions. In short, from being a mechanical device for restricting government by dividing the exercise of its powers between its various specific activities, the 'separation of powers' has come to be understood as a principle embodying a suspicion of all great concentrations of power, that of government among them.

The politics of scepticism has understood its contemporary business to be: first, to detect what is afoot; secondly to perceive the manner in which government can perform most economically its perennial office of preserving an order and balance relevant to the current condition and activities of the society; and, thirdly, to recall political activity to this pursuit and turn its inventiveness in this direction.

The pull of faith has led to the emergence of massive assemblies of power. Modern government itself is chief among these; and where this is not defended merely on account of the 'good' that may be expected to spring from it, it is excused on the pseudo-sceptical ground that in a general increase in power a large share must be appropriated to government in order that the rest may be controlled. And in addition, political activity has been forced into narrow channels, its attention riveted upon the current project while the large displacements which follow from this concentration of purpose have been overlooked or insufficiently considered. The distant future has attracted disproportionate attention, and activity being stretched always to its fullest extent, no reserve is left to meet the unavoidable emergencies.[16]

In the sceptic's reading of the situation, then, what needs to be restored in contemporary politics is a balance of attention and a balance of power. For example, a condition in which activity is determined wholly by the past, or the present, or the future is recognized as being unbalanced. And, in this connection, the imbalance of contemporary politics springs from the preoccupation with the future which has been pressed upon it by the politics of faith, and which threatens to destroy the continuity of activity by destroying our sympathy with its earlier enterprise. And in order to restore the balance, what needs to be promoted

---

[16] I think it is not unjust to hold overlong preoccupation with the politics of faith responsible for our being morally unprepared for the emergence of those forms of power known as the internal combustion engine and atomic energy. This understanding of politics sees every accession of power as *prima facie* 'good'; and when a particular accession of power proves dangerous, the habit of faith is to suppose that the danger can be averted by a piece of *ad hoc* political machinery. Faith is hostile to that steady reserve of scepticism which alone is capable of mediating change and controlling it, not merely when it has taken place, but while it is taking place and before it has reached unmanageable proportions.

is the understanding of politics as a conversation in which past, present and future each has a voice; and while one or other of them may on occasion properly prevail, none is given exclusive attention.

Again, the uncritical welcome which the politics of faith has given to every fresh addition to our power to control men and things and to exploit the world (a welcome determined almost exclusively by considerations of economic prosperity) has assembled great and almost sovereign concentrations of power and has transformed the normal tensions of society into a war of giants. A balance of power has become impossible because, with the destruction of the smaller make-weights, only the massive weights remain, and consequently the scale bumps crudely from side to side. And, as the sceptic understands it, in order to restore the possibility of an equilibrium, the power available needs to be redispersed in its exercise among a multitude of semi-independencies (among them the individual subject protected in his semi-independence by a right to private property as little qualified as may be), none of them (not even government) enjoying enough power to impose a single and comprehensive pattern of activity upon the society.

Moreover, the sceptic is aware that the balance of a society in which power is distributed in its exercise among a great number of beneficiaries is always precarious. Arrangements which in their beginning promote a dispersal of power often, in the course of time, come to create over-mighty or even absolute combinations, alliances or institutions, while continuing to claim the recognition and loyalty which belonged to them in their first character. We need to be clear-sighted enough to recognize such a change and energetic enough to set on foot a remedy while the imbalance is still small. And what more than anything else contributes to this clear-sightedness is relief from the distraction of a rigid doctrine which fixes upon an arrangement a falsely permanent character. The best institutions, in the judgement of the sceptic, are those whose character is both firm and self-critical, recognizing themselves as the repository of a beneficial fragment of power, but refusing the inevitable invitation to absolutism. But institutions, like persons, must always be expected to overreach themselves, and the office of government is to maintain the balance by keeping them in their place.

In these circumstances, it might be thought that government would need to be endowed with extraordinary power, capable of holding all other powers and assemblies of power in check. But this is not the view which the sceptic will be disposed to take. In his reading of human behaviour there is no more reason to expect that men engaged in the activity of governing will be more moderate than those who pursue other activities, and no less reason to anticipate imbalance from the immoderation of governors than from the immoderation of anyone else. In his understanding, then, the power necessary to govern is more economically collected from the absence of great competing assemblies of power than from the enjoyment of overwhelming power in a world composed of great powers. For overwhelming power would be required only by a government which had against it a combination so extensive of the powers enjoyed by such a variety of different individuals and interests as to convict the government of a self-interest so gross as to disqualify it for the performance of its proper office. Normally government requires to be assured of only a power greater than that which is assembled in any one other centre of power on any particular occasion.

But further, the sceptic observes in what is called the 'rule of law' a manner of governing remarkably economical in its use of power and consequently one that wins his approval. If the activity of governing were the continuous or sporadic interruption of the habits and arrangements of society, even with arbitrary corrective measures (to say nothing of measures designed to impose a single pattern upon activity), extraordinary power would be required, each of its acts being an *ad hoc* intervention; and in addition, in spite of this extraordinary power in the hands of government, the society would be without any known and protective structure exerting a continuous containing pressure upon the forces of dissolution. But government by rule of law (that is, by means of the enforcement by prescribed methods of settled rules binding alike on governors and governed), while losing nothing in strength, is itself an emblem of that diffusion of power which it exists to promote. It is the method of governing most economical in the use of power: it involves a partnership between past and present and between governors and governed which leaves no room for arbitrariness; it encourages a tradition of moderation and of resistance to the growth of dangerous assemblies of power which is far more effective than any promiscuous onslaught, however crushing; it controls effectively, but without breaking the grand affirmative flow of activity; and it gives a practical definition of the kind of limited but necessary service that may be expected from government, restraining us from vain and dangerous expectation, and it from overreaching ambition. And if in the end the contemporary sceptic returns to the doctrine of the 'separation of powers' in the more formal sense, it will be to observe not only the benefit to be derived from the maintenance of some measure of independence for each of the specific 'powers of government', but also the appropriateness of a manner of governing in which power is shared conversationally between a multitude of different interests, persons and offices, government appearing, for example, as a partnership between a cabinet and the members of a representative assembly, between a minister and a permanent official and perhaps between assemblies representative of different interests.

What strength a sceptical style of politics of this kind may have in contemporary political activity may be assessed by those who think they know how to assess it. It cannot be said to be the tide upon which our politics is at present riding. But the history of our politics in the last hundred and fifty years would have been very different from what in fact it has been if the pull of political scepticism had been either absent or weak. In so far as this history has been the story not of the promotion of rapid change or the imposition of a comprehensive pattern of activity, but of a succession of political expedients to mediate current changes, to secure workable arrangements and to remove manifest disequilibriums; in so far as speculative ideas and large ambitions have played a subordinate part; in so far as changes have not been pressed to their so-called 'logical' conclusions and the impulse to 'symmetry' has been kept within reasonable bounds; and in so far as abrupt transitions have been avoided and faith in magic transformations and visionary enterprises has been moderated, the politics of scepticism, [in these,] if in no other respects, has made itself felt. But its inspiration, at least in England, has never been merely an opposition to the politics of faith, but an understanding of the office of government, elicited for the most part from some of the ancient traditions of English politics, patiently considered and reconsidered in each generation and applied to the current situations of the modern world.

5

THE NEMESIS OF FAITH
AND SCEPTICISM

I

The distinctive nature of modern European political activity and understanding (I have contended) is the potentiality of internal movement which they derive from their heterogeneous and complex character. And I have maintained that the historic poles of this movement are the two extremes which I have called the politics of faith and the politics of scepticism. Further, in so far as our political activity has on occasion come near to being immobilized at either of these extremes, or in so far as it has been turned decisively in the direction of either of them, two opposed styles of governing and understanding the office of government have been intimated or have even appeared. And since our political activity has always been turned in one or other of these directions and has never for long taken one direction without being recalled by the pull exercised by the other pole, it may be described, from different points of view, either as a fluctuation between two historic poles, or as a *concordia discors* of two opposed styles of government. Finally, I have suggested that the notorious ambiguity of our political language springs not from any temporary or disingenuous corruption of a once unequivocal vocabulary, but from the fact that, at whatever point we find ourselves in the range of internal movement potential in our politics, we have at our disposal one and the same set of words in which to express these diverse understandings of the activity of governing. In short, this ambiguity is specific and not merely general. And since its specific character derives from the specific character of the extremes between which we move, we must consider the precise polarity of our politics in order to understand it. And the more thoroughly we consider the character of these extremes, the clearer will be our view of the predicament of modern politics.

Each of these opposed styles of politics, when taken by itself, may be said to provoke a characteristic nemesis. But in neither case is the nemesis an external condemnation of the style, nor is it merely a fate which may be expected to overtake it if it persists in its ways. No doubt it is some dim perception of what lies in wait for our politics at each of its horizons that has kept us from a final surrender to either; but that is not what I am considering. The nemesis I speak of is, in each of these styles of politics, a confession or revelation of its own character. And consequently to investigate it is not merely to feed our apprehension of what might happen if our political activity were to become immobilized at either of these extremes; it is to reach a clearer understanding of the extremes themselves.

Each of these styles in its concrete appearances in political activity, and even in its appearances in the writings of its adherents, is qualified by the occasion of its appearance. Neither has ever filled our world of politics to the exclusion of the other; each has always been disguised with ornaments borrowed from its opponent, diluted by reminiscences of a character it assumed in order to defend itself on a particular occasion, or qualified by the contingent characteristics of some temporary version of itself. Nevertheless, each of these styles may be said to have an uninhibited character – a character which would reveal itself if the style stood alone, but which is never fully revealed so long as it appears in company with its opponent. And I speak of this uninhibited character as the nemesis of the style, because in each case it turns out to be a self-destructive character. When our political vocabulary becomes a vocabulary exclusive either to faith or to scepticism, the words at once lose their ambiguity, but at the same time they represent and suggest directions of political activity which if pursued defeat themselves. This, indeed, is what we should expect; it both repeats and confirms the reading of the extremes of our politics as the poles of a single activity and not as mere alternative opposites each capable of providing a concrete manner of governing and a coherent understanding of government. And it confirms also the reading of the ambiguity, not as a regrettable corruption of language, but as a characteristic of our politics without which they would be wholly different from what they are. In short, when either of these styles of politics claims for itself independence and completeness, it reveals a self-defeating character. Each is not less the partner than the opponent of the other; each stands in need of the other to rescue it from self-destruction, and if either succeeded in destroying the other, it would discover that, in the same act, it had destroyed itself.

The uninhibited character of each of these two styles of politics has, then, to be extricated. And to do this is not a purely logical exercise. It is true that each is a system, and from this point of view the nemesis is the incoherence of the system. Nevertheless, what we have to observe is not merely logical inconsistencies, nor is it merely a discrepancy between the ends and the means proposed; it is the manner in which each style, when relieved of the modifying partnership of its opponent, defeats its own purposes. And to elicit this is an imaginative rather than a logical exercise. Whenever the politics of modern Europe have moved decisively in the direction of either of these extremes, the shadow of the nemesis has appeared: our task is to reconstruct from these shadowy intimations the hidden character, or at least the hidden characteristics, which they signify.

II

The situtation we have to consider in relation to each of these styles of politics is this. A society is a complex of activities. And the societies of modern Europe are distinguished by the great variety of the activities which compose them. Even if we may discern a few main directions of activity, each of these itself exhibits great internal variety of pursuit, and none is so far dominant as to put the others out of business. No societies have been less monolithic in their activities than those of modern Europe. Government, on the other hand, is a small body of men, usually occupying recognized offices, authorized in some recognized manner and empowered to control the activities of its subjects. The manner in which this control is exercised distinguishes one style of government from another.

In the politics of faith, governing is the minute and comprehensive control of all activities. The office of government is recognized as the imposition and maintenance of a condition of human circumstance in which all the activities afoot are made to conform to a single pattern or are set in one direction: those incapable of conforming are properly eliminated. The direction imposed may reveal itself in a rational consideration of the current directions of activity and may be selected because it appears to be already dominant. It may, on the other hand, be the product of a visionary experience of what is proper to mankind. Again, the chosen direction may impose itself gradually, or it may be imposed in a revolutionary manner. But whatever the manner of its appearance and imposition, it is unavoidably one of the directions of activity already intimated in the society upon which it is to be imposed: government, in this style, is never imposition of an entirely fresh direction of activity. Even the 'righteousness', which it was the office of the rule of the 'saints' to impose, was already recognized among the current directions of activity in seventeenth-century England. Further, the direction is chosen because it is believed to be preeminently proper to mankind and consequently to attract to itself the epithet 'perfect'. And until this direction is determined, the work of government (which is to impose and maintain it) cannot, properly speaking, begin.

Governing, then, in this understanding of it, is a 'total' activity. And this means that every permitted activity is itself an activity of governing (and is recognized as such), and that every subject legitimately employed is *eo ipso* an agent of government. The situation here is not that the appointed agents of government are expected to be everywhere in control of every activity; this may indeed be so, but it is not the significant point. The situation is that to be legitimately active is itself to be doing the work which, in this understanding of it, is the work of government. For every manner of activity must be understood either to be participation in the establishment and maintenance of the chosen condition of human circumstance (which is participation in the task assigned to government), or to be illegitimate. There is, then, in such a community only one work being carried on; and the various manners in which it may be pursued (sleeping, agriculture, painting pictures, nurturing children, etc.) are not distinct and independent activities, they are the indistinct components of a single pattern. What exists (for example) is not 'football', but 'football-in-so-far-as-it-promotes-perfection'. And the threefold division of activities possible elsewhere – governing, going about one's lawful business, and behaving unlawfully – is reduced to two by the coalescence of the first and second.

Moreover, the same conclusion appears when the situation is considered from the other end. For example, in that version of the politics of faith for which the maximum exploitation of the resources of the world is the 'perfection' pursued, a community is appropriately recognized as a 'factory'. A subject is recognized as an 'employee' in the enterprise of 'perfection'; all legitimate activity is understood as 'factory work'. And since the activity of governing cannot be made an exception to this without being made illegitimate, what distinguishes a community of this sort is a single comprehensive manner of activity. In short, government in the service of 'perfection' appears not as a style of politics, but as a manner of abolishing politics. This, indeed, is the nemesis we should expect. In the politics of faith, each word in our political vocabulary (the word 'government' included) acquires a maximum meaning appropriate to the 'perfection' pursued, and enjoying that maximum meaning it comes to stand for all forms of legitimate activity and so none in particular.[1]

Politics, then, as the pursuit of perfection, when they are out of reach of any modifying agency, are unable to protect themselves from dissolution. When government is understood as an activity of limitless control, it finds itself with nothing to control: a *factotum* has no subjects who are not opponents. This self-destruction is inherent in the uninhibited character of the politics of faith. But it is illustrated, and perhaps reinforced, in a number of contingent defects, some of which rank as self-defeats.

---

[1] 'Government . . . has no special character.' Leon Duguit, *Law and the Modern State* (tr. Laski), p. 49. This nemesis is intimated in many features of the manner of life enjoyed whenever and wherever our politics has touched the horizon of faith. On these occasions what has appropriately appeared is not merely the minute control of all activities which we associate with 'bureaucracy' or a *Beamtenstaat*, nor is it merely a multiplicity of informers, but the destruction of politics by the conversion of every activity into a 'political' activity and of every subject into an agent of government. And there is no end to the reverberations of this *motif* - unless the request of a wife for her husband to be executed for illegitimate activity may be said to be an 'end'. But it begins in far less spectacular appearances. It is present, for example, in the confusion of mind which overtakes those who speak the language of this style. For example, Lindsay (*Essentials of Democracy*, p. 7) and others who speak of the 'democratization of industry' can evidently observe no distinction between 'government' and the management of industry. And the view that the pursuit of 'perfection' is a *techne* which is all-inclusive and consequently that a farmer, a scientist, a composer or a mother, if they are proficient in this one *techne* are qualified to carry on their business, is an unfortunate (though legitimate) child of the politics of faith.

In a community whose members, engaged in few activities and those of the simplest character, are not drawn in a variety of directions, the politics of faith will have some appropriateness. Indeed, a monolithic society may be expected to have a monolithic politics. And where there is only a single direction available, it will be followed, not because it is perceived to be the road to 'perfection', but because no alternative presents itself. But the characteristic of the communities of modern Europe is the multiplicity of their activities and directions of activity. And in this historic situation, the politics of faith, in which a single direction is selected for pursuit, all others being proscribed, has an incongruous appearance. It is a style of government at variance with the structure of the community it governs: it demands an exclusive direction of activity from subjects who do not readily recognize the relevance of the demand. Consequently, in the conditions of modern Europe, government in this style is engaged on a double task: first, of subduing the society, and secondly, of maintaining its submission to a single direction of activity. And to perform these tasks it will have need of immense power and will be incited to a continuous search for greater and greater quantities of power. But the more power it acquires, and indeed the more successful it appears in subduing the diverse activities to one activity, the more closely it will come to resemble an alien authority, until in the end it reveals itself (in respect of its power and its hostility) as comparable to a 'force of nature'. And a people whose activity is being directed, and being ever more thoroughly directed, to the conquest of nature and the exploitation of its resources, will recognize such a force as something it has been taught to oppose, or at least outwit. Thus the operation of one of the versions of the politics of faith, in the circumstances of modern Europe, may be seen to defeat itself by adding one more direction of activity to the already multiple directions, namely, the search for imprecisions in the pattern, the profitless activity of circumventing the minute control it is endeavouring to impose. Nor is this kind of self-destruction merely speculative; it has its parallels in the other versions of the politics of faith, and wherever this style of government has in any degree begun to impose itself upon the diverse activities of a modern European community, its shadow has appeared. It is the *impasse* which awakens the politics of Terror which sleeps in every version of government as the pursuit of 'perfection' when it is imposed upon an already diverse community.

The condition of human circumstance selected for exclusive

pursuit in the politics of faith is, we have seen, collected in some manner from the community upon which it is to be imposed by government. The pattern of 'perfection' is one of the current directions of activity: it is an historic direction. The Baconian 'exploitation of the resources of the world', the 'righteousness' of the seventeenth-century 'saints' and the more recent direction of 'security', each belong to a particular historic context, and it is this context which gives them their specific character and plausibility. But in the politics of faith the exclusive conditions of human circumstance must be pursued as if its validity were permanent, not merely historical. Everything in this style of government is appropriately built to last; where the design of 'perfection' has been discovered, change need neither be feared nor anticipated, and what is unshakable is preferred to what is recognized as ephemeral. Where the proper direction of activity has been determined, there is no wisdom (only folly) in providing against mistakes by making tentative engagements and gradual explorations.[2] In this sense the politics of faith is the politics of immortality; the point of no-return cannot be reached too quickly and is recognized not with misgiving but with enthusiasm. In the conduct of affairs this style of government always backs the favourite, never the field. And buoyed up with certainty (the self-righteousness of the 'saint' and the self-confidence of the Baconian are in this respect twins) the politician of faith is appropriately prepared to risk everything for the fabulous prize of 'perfection'. But in fact the condition of human circumstance he pursues has no such permanent significance. It is composed of nothing more substantial than the perceptions of fallible intelligences dramatized by the passions of a few generations: in contemporary politics alone there are at least two versions of 'perfection' which compete with one another. Consequently, the imperishable monuments of the politics of faith are imperishable ruins, 'follies' remarkable often for the strength of their materials and always for the eccentricity of their design. That jealousy of time which faith proclaims, not only in its pretence of finality, but also in its characteristic urgency, is, in fact, a proclamation of self-defeat.

Moreover, if there is one nemesis reserved for the pretence of finality in politics, there is another which follows upon the pre-

---

[2] The Education Act of 1944 is deeply veined with the politics of faith, and some of its provisions are being riveted upon us by school buildings which are exclusively appropriate to them.

occupation with the future which is characteristic of the politics of faith. Government as the minute direction of every activity in pursuit of a condition of human circumstance called (and perhaps universally agreed to be) 'perfection' shoulders a tremendous responsibility. The appropriate attitude of the subject cannot be one of indifference, or tolerance, or even mere approval; it must be an attitude of devotion, of gratitude and of love. The zeal for 'perfection' which belongs to this style of government (and was early observed to do so by Halifax and Hume) has its counterpart in the enthusiasm of the subject for his government. The enemies of a regime will be identified not as mere dissidents to be inhibited, but as unbelievers to be converted. Mere obedience is not enough; it must be accompanied by fervour.[3] Indeed, if the subject is not enthusiastic about government there is no legitimate object for his devotion; if he is devoted to 'perfection' he *must* be devoted to government. And whenever our politics has turned decisively in the direction of the horizon of faith, government has always demanded not acquiescence but love and devotion. But in these circumstances, where what is promised is 'salvation', the achievement of government must always be either too great or too small, and in both cases gratitude is turned into hatred, and the self-defeating character of the style reveals itself.

Suppose (what has never yet happened) that this style of government were to establish a condition of human circumstances recognized as 'perfection'. Many disconcerting consequences would follow, and not least among them this: the subject would owe (and would be aware of owing) everything he could value to a single benefactor. But finding himself without the means of requiting this debt (which he sees to comprise all his indebtedness), his joy will make itself known as misery and his gratitude as animosity. For, as Tacitus observes: 'benefits received are a delight to us as long as we think we can requite them; when that possibility is far exceeded, they are repaid with hatred instead of gratitude.'[4]

On the other hand, let us suppose (a more likely occurrence)

---

[3] The Greek muleteer who, when asked why he beat his animal, which was going very well, replied, 'Yes, but he doesn't *want* to go,' was an exponent of the politics of faith. This is Pascal's definition of tyranny. *Pensées* (Brunschvicg), p. 332.

[4] *Ann.* iv. 18. cf. Montaigne, *Essais*, ii. 12; Pascal, *Pensées*, 72; La Rochefoucauld, *Maximes*, 226.

that, promising 'perfection', this style of government finds it difficult to fulfil its undertaking, or manifestly falls far short. It has aroused desires which it is unable to satisfy, or to satisfy immediately. In these circumstances, the attention of the subject will be directed to the future, and at the same time government will bend itself with fresh energy to the task. But on both accounts it will forfeit the love and devotion it demands.

In respect of the first, government will address itself thus to the subject: 'You are to know that perfection is a great prize, difficult to win. We are on the way to it; but it is unreasonable to expect the mess of ages suddenly to be transformed into para- dise.[5] And you are to know also that although you may not live to enter the promised land, your children and your children's children will inhabit it. What you lack, they will enjoy. To you will belong the undying glory that attaches to pioneers.' And to these comforting words the subject will respond with due gratitude. He will be capable (it may be supposed) of making do with less than 'perfection' so long as his confidence that it is on the way is not shaken. For a period he may be satisfied with the dim com- fort of distant utopias.

But in respect of the second, government in this style will speak as follows: 'The pursuit of "perfection" is an arduous undertaking. You must not only expect to forego delights which those who come after will enjoy, you must also expect to suffer the pains and deprivations inseparable from the enterprise. We are responsible for leading you towards the promised land, and we cannot discharge this duty without plenary powers. We require, not a "doctor's mandate", but a "saviour's mandate". But do not allow the sufferings of this present time, or even some of the rather odd demands we must make of you, to disturb your confidence. Be assured that we recognize only one duty, the duty to "perfect" mankind; and we will allow nothing to stand in the way of its performance.'

And with this proclamation will appear on the surface all that lies hidden in the recesses of this style of politics: a character scarcely calculated to inspire devotion. Every protective for- mality in the conduct of affairs will be recognized as an impedi- ment to the pursuit of 'perfection', the antinomian character which belongs to all activity tied to a single overmastering prin- ciple will appear; engagements, loyalties, undertakings will be

---

[5] 'Heaven can be established on earth.' Lenin, *The Threatened Catastrophe.*

swept aside; actual miseries (in this crow's flight to 'perfection') will be overlooked or discounted; prayers will be offered for 'industrial peace' (so that we can get on with the job), while the poor, the oppressed, the terrorized and the tortured are forgotten; no price will be considered too high to pay for 'perfection'. Indeed, an *interimsethik* will be announced: a temporary transvaluation of values in which the 'perfection' of mankind will be seen to spring from the degradation of living men. The present, represented as an interlude between night and day, will become an uncertain twilight.[6] Compassion will be treason, love heresy. And in these circumstances, where *il n'y a que de cadavres ou de demi-dieux*, where it will be difficult to hide the slaughter and impossible to conceal the corruption, and where the ship is so conspicuously preferred to the crew, it is not unlikely that gratitude and devotion will be reserved. In success, then, and in failure, and always when it is in process, government as the pursuit of 'perfection', when it stands alone, is a self-defeating style of politics. It requires what it cannot command, and needs what its character prohibits.

The nemesis of faith, then, is the manner in which government, when harnessed to the pursuit of 'perfection', unavoidably collapses: the engagement to impose a single pattern of activity upon a community is a self-defeating engagement. And this is further illustrated in what may be called the logic of 'security' in the politics of faith.

There is a critical point in the scale of meanings which belong to the word 'security' in a political vocabulary. On one side of this point, protection against some of the vicissitudes of fortune is recognized to be among the activities of government. Here the inspiration is the observation of actual miseries suffered; and 'security' is understood as the assurance of relief. Nevertheless, the range of this assurance is not determined by the magnitude of the misery, but by a perception of the displacements consequent upon its removal. Any 'protection' involves government taking charge of some of the activities of the subject; but the limit here is the 'protection' which can be supplied without imposing a comprehensive pattern of activity upon the commu-

---

[6] In this twilight, doctors will dream of the rapid advances that might be made in medicine if they were supplied with expendable human subjects for experiment. And philanthropists, like Robert Owen, will recognize in the poor admirable material for social experiment, because they are unable to defend themselves.

nity. When a man is defended against misfortune in such a way as to deprive him of the authority to defend himself, the limit is passed.

On the other side of this point, however, 'security' is understood to mean the assurance of a certain level of 'well-being', and government is understood to be the activity of providing this assurance. In general, the politics of faith may be said to begin at this point, where the minimum meanings of 'security' begin to turn into the maximum. But only in one of its versions is 'security' recognized as itself the comprehensive direction of activity to be imposed upon the community, and consequently it is there that the nemesis of 'security' is to be perceived. And since what is sought is not merely 'protection' against some of the vicissitudes of fortune, but a community organized expressly for the exclusion of vicissitude, the most minute and relentless control of all activities will be called for. The first need of government is, consequently, immense power; and it will be supposed that the assurance the subject has of enjoying this condition of 'security' will be proportionate to the power at the disposal of government. The unsought (but nevertheless unavoidable) accompaniments of this style of government have often been pointed out. Where 'perfection' is identified with 'security' the common condition of the subject will be one of slavery qualified by whatever privilege he can secure for himself by an even more prostrate submission; and the condition of the community will be the enjoyment of an ever decreasing level of well-being as the motive for exertion slackens. But these consequences are costs within his power to pay; to some they may seem intolerable, but they do not amount to the self-defeat of the style of government. Nevertheless this is a self-destructive style of government; and the shadow of this self-destruction has hung over Europe for some generations. For, while it is true that complete insulation from vicissitude is impossible without government endowed with immense power, it is also true that where government possesses this immense power, 'security' at once diminishes: the condition of absolute 'security' is a condition also of absolute precariousness.

The mechanism of self-defeat may be elucidated in this manner. A man in Anglo-Norman England, harassed by insecurity, might commend himself to a powerful magnate and thus win protection from some of the vicissitudes of fortune. Obligations would be entailed, and these would appear on the balance-sheet as small additions to the power of the magnate. But the practical conditions on which commendation could increase the security of the client were that the power of the magnate was great, but not boundless, and that the contribution to this power made by each client was small, but not insignificant. For if to commend himself were to tie himself to the mighty ambitions which accompany immense power, the client might find himself secured against many of the minor vicissitudes of life but at the same time a partner in larger struggles and a prey to larger vicissitudes in which he had hitherto no share, and indeed which would not exist (or would exist only on a smaller scale) if he and his like did not make their contributions to the power of the magnate.

In principle, then, the price of 'security' is submission. And while a certain level of 'security' may be enjoyed by an appropriate submission to a moderately powerful protector, it would seem that a comprehensive 'security' might be achieved by a total submission to an immensely powerful protector. This, indeed, is the inference involved in this version of the politics of faith. For here, all subjects are commended to one protector, the government, and the immense power thus generated is available to be brought to bear whenever any item in this comprehensive 'security' is threatened. But the result is different from what was anticipated. Where every activity is an activity of government, the opportunities of conflict between communities organized for this kind of 'security' are enormously increased in number and the occasions in severity. Indeed, a world of communities each organized for comprehensive 'security' is a world organized for dispute, and (since the whole power of the community is behind every dispute) for major dispute. No community can, in fact, enjoy comprehensive security without so great a command over the affairs of so many other communities that, where submission is not immediately forthcoming, conflict is unavoidable. Unless what is to be secured is a level of 'well-being' below that which is currently enjoyed, to defend 'security' in one place must be to attack it elsewhere. In short, the version of the politics of faith in which 'perfection' is identified with 'security' is a style of politics which calls for government with a greater endowment of power than any other, and it is one in which power is more easily and more plausibly collected than in any other. But whatever minor protections and securities it may provide, the unavoidable product of this immense and ever active concentration of power, directed to the achievement of this purpose, is a diminished security and an enlarged precariousness.

There is, it is true, a passage in the myth of this version of the politics of faith designed to provide against this contingency. It was believed that if 'the people' (that is, 'the masses' from whose submissiveness government derives its power to dispense a comprehensive 'security') were to remain in control of the power generated by their submissiveness, then the nemesis of 'security' would be avoided. War was represented as the sport of kings; and a people submissive only to its own government would never be tricked out of the enjoyment of what it had provided the means to establish. But this escape from the nemesis of 'security' has proved itself an illusion. No community can enjoy comprehensive 'security' without a comprehensive mastery of the world, and no subject can enjoy comprehensive security without complete submissiveness to a power great enough to win that mastery. Moreover, government is not only a set of arrangements for the discharge of public business, in this case the provision of comprehensive 'security'; it is also what J. S. Mill called 'a great influence acting upon the human mind'. Where to govern is to wield immense power, the activity of governing attracts to its service not men of moderation and self-control concerned to avoid the defects of the enterprise upon which they are engaged, but either the neurotic and the frustrated who know no bounds or the parvenu who is easily intoxicated by the chance of doing big and clever things. And where this power is generated from the submissiveness of 'the masses' in search of comprehensive 'security', it falls into the hands of protectors who promise more than they can perform and, pretending to lead, impose the responsibility for their actions upon their followers.[7] Indeed, it is only the reminiscence of the moderation which belongs to the minimum meaning of 'security' which makes the politics of the maximum meaning seem even plausible. Or, alternatively, it is only when the pull of scepticism is exerted upon this version of faith that self-defeat is avoided.

---

[7] 'The choice was put to them, whether they would like to be kings or kings' couriers. Like children, they all wanted to be couriers. So now there are a great many couriers, they post through the world, and, as there are no kings left, shout to each other their meaningless and obsolete messages. They would gladly put an end to their wretched lives, but they dare not because of their oaths of service.' Kafka, *Aphorisms*.

There is one other aspect of the nemesis of the politics of faith to be considered, namely, what may be called its moral infirmity. For although this infirmity does not itself involve self-defeat, it must nevertheless be counted a quality on account of which the style is incapable of standing by itself.

A moral activity is one in which a principle of self-limitation is detectable; merely to respond to the push of circumstance may on occasion be unavoidable, but it is something less than being morally active. The components whose relationship we have to consider here are the power available to government and the enterprise of imposing a single pattern of activity, and with it a monolithic character, upon a community. And our question is whether the politics of faith should be understood as a speculative idea supplying itself (or being providentially supplied) with the necessary power, and therefore enjoying a principle of self-limitation; or whether they should be understood as merely an excess of power inciting government to engage in the limitless activity of pursuing 'perfection'. For merely to respond to the incitement of power, to follow wherever it leads and to exploit every enlargement, is not a moral activity; it is only a display of energy. If this were a question of precedence, there is no doubt about what our answer must be. To impose a single pattern of activity upon a community (and moreover upon a community distinguished by a new-found multiplicity of directions of activity) requires a minute and relentless control which only a government endowed with great power could even contemplate. And not until governments were long practiced in the enterprise of minute control, undertaken gradually and often for the immediate purpose of victory in war,[8] did the notion of minute control in pursuit of 'perfection' emerge. But it is not a question of precedence; our problem is whether the idea of 'perfection' is capable of supplying a principle of self-limitation and thus transforming a display of energy into a moral activity. And the answer appears to be that the idea of 'perfection' in virtue of its own limitlessness is incapable of self-limitation. To impose and maintain a single pattern of activity (not for some limited purpose, such as victory in war, but because this pattern of activity is

---

[8] cf. *Cambridge Economic History of Europe*, vol. II, ch. vii, p. 9. [The reference to the *Cambridge Economic History of Europe* is a mistake. The reference is actually to Lionel Robbins, *The Theory of Economic Policy, in English Classical Political Economy* (London: Macmillan, 1952). See Editor's Introduction above, p. ix.]

recognized to be the 'perfect' condition of human circumstance) is in itself indistinguishable from bringing to bear upon the community all the power available to government and engaging in a perpetual search for more and more extensive power. It does not call for a quantum of power appropriate to the achievement of a specific purpose: the purpose is in the custody of the power and extends with every extension of power.[9]

It seems, then, that the politics of faith is the pursuit of 'perfection' harnessed to power: the character of 'perfection' being merely that condition of human circumstance which emerges when minute and relentless control is exercised over the activities of the subject. Nor is it remarkable that this should be so. Many of our activities are of this kind, the work being inspired by the tools which are themselves gradually improved as the project goes forward and merely as a means of forwarding the project. The production of wealth, for example, which, while it may be limited by considerations of enjoyment, may also become a habit which far outruns this limit and acquires a momentum of its own directed towards a maximum which coincides with a diminished rather than an enhanced happiness. And both the extension of 'education' in the last hundred and fifty years, and the enlargement of the activities of the BBC from its small beginnings, are examples of the same process at work. But what is remarkable is the manner in which such enterprises are endowed with a spurious moral character on account, it would seem, of the energy and persistence with which they are pursued, and even on account of the appearance they have of inevitability when they are properly under way. So far, then, the politics of faith are comparable to the exploitation of a technique; impelled by an inner momentum, they are as little hindered as may be by considerations even of utility and are devoid of any principle of self-limitation.

But this is not the end of the matter. The politics of faith appear not in general, but in a variety of versions; and it belongs to a version to supply a principle of self-limitation. 'Perfection' is not merely what appears when minute and relentless control is taken of all the activities of the subject: it is a mundane condition of human circumstances which has suffered definition. What is

---

[9] 'It is the duty of government to do whatever is conducive to the welfare of the governed. The only limit to this duty is power . . .' Nassau Senior, quoted in Robbins, op. cit., p. 45.

sought is 'righteousness', or 'the maximum exploitation of the resources of the world', or 'security'. Here 'perfection' is not harnessed to power; power is harnessed to particularized 'perfection'. And in so far as these notions of 'perfection' are exclusive of one another, there would appear to be in each a principle of self-limitation. Nevertheless, the appearance is illusory. If 'righteousness', or 'the maximum exploitation of the resources of the world', or 'security' were understood as limited objectives, each calling for an appropriate (and therefore limited) supply of power for its achievement, then each would certainly enjoy a principle of self-limitation. But in the politics of faith this is not so. They are exclusive notions of 'perfection', not alternative forms of 'perfection', because *ex hypothesi* 'perfection' cannot have alternative forms. And appearing as notions of 'perfection', they do not each call for a different and appropriate supply of power; they each call for as much as there is and for the endless search for more, and in doing so share a common limitless character. In short, the distinctions which the various versions of the politics of faith appear to represent are distinctions without differences. Each is defined, not by itself, but by the power available or in prospect; each is an activity to be 'moralized' only on the principle 'I ought because I can.' And, paradoxically, as it will seem to some, it is their character as 'perfection' which turns their pursuit from a moral activity into a mere response to the incitement of power.

III

The nemesis of sceptical politics, when they are freed from any modifying agency, is less spectacular than that of the politics of faith in similar circumstances: the self-defeat of scepticism is both less devastating and more subtle. And this difference of standing between the two styles (which has already suggested itself at other points in our investigation) is not insignificant; it represents a principle which must be considered later in more detail. Nevertheless, self-defeat is not absent from the politics of scepticism: to say the least, it is unsteady when it stands by itself.

The sceptical style of government is not anarchical: the extreme here is not 'no-government', or even government reduced to the smallest dimensions. Faith reveals itself as maximum government, the total ordering of the activities of the subject, and, from this point of view, scepticism may be said to represent minimum government: it is concerned to impose the least possible uniformity upon the direction of activity. But the character of the sceptical style is not merely what it is when reflected in the mirror of faith. It has a positive office, the maintenance of a relevant public order in a community; and it can rise above minimum government, and be imperial in its own province, without approximating itself to rule in the manner of faith. Consequently the nemesis here is not the absence of government, nor is it an inclination towards weak government. Indeed, in its characteristic sphere of activity, and on account of the narrowness of that sphere, government in the sceptical style is able to be strong just where the government of faith is liable to be weak. The power it needs, since it is not great, is (in modern times) readily available; the manner in which this power is used does not provoke massive opposition which calls for great and possibly insufficient exertions; and because in normal circumstances this style of government is never at the end of its tether, there remains always something in hand for occasions of emergency. In short, this style of government can be strong because it does not need to be overwhelming in order to be strong: it is paramount because its activities are limited.

In the politics of faith, government has no special character. On this account it becomes, in the end, the only legitimate activity; and, in general, the nemesis of this style springs from its characteristic limitlessness, its concern with 'perfection'. In the politics of scepticism, on the other hand, government appears as one among the many forms of activity which compose a community; it is preeminent only in respect of being concerned with a universal aspect of activities, namely, their disposition to limit one another. And, in general, the nemesis of scepticism springs from the severe self-limitation which belongs to its character. Its office is to maintain a relevant public order, that is, an order appropriate to the manner and directions of the activities which compose the community. But the habit of being exact, and never excessive, in the performance of this duty is apt to make the performance itself less ready. And, in this respect, when it stands alone, the politics of scepticism reveal a certain inappropriateness to the conditions of modern European communities.

Government in the manner of faith must be and seems to be a hostile power in any community save one engaged in few and simple activities. Consequently it has the appearance of an intruder in the communities of modern Europe: its first duty is to impose simplicity, to reduce activities to those which can be controlled by the power available. But what is characteristic of these communities is not only a multiplicity of directions of activity, but also a disposition for rapid and perpetual change. And an appropriate manner of government will be one which not only recognizes multiplicity but one that is also alive to change. It is at this point that the characteristic failure of the politics of scepticism appears: it is a style of government preeminently suitable for a complex but relatively static condition of society. The government of faith is alive to change because its chief office is to suppress change where it involves divergence from the chosen direction of 'perfection', and there is nothing in its character which stands in the way of its carrying out this duty. The government of scepticism, on the other hand, having no authority to prevent it, is relatively indifferent to change of any kind, and consequently is apt to be insensitive even to those effects of change which come within its province, namely the appearance of conditions which require an adjustment in the system of rights and duties if a relevant order is to be maintained. Nor is this a contingent failing: it is a defect of the virtue of this style of government.

A community given to rapid and perpetual change in the directions of its activities stands in particular need of a manner of government not itself readily involved in change. And the insistence on formality, as an emblem of orderliness in the maintenance of order, which belongs to scepticism, is clearly appropriate. But the reluctance to jeopardize order by a ready resort to informality has its counterpart in a resistance to those modifications of formalities without which order rapidly becomes irrelevant and consequently self-destructive. And where (as here) virtue lies, not in imagining and anticipating change, but in devising the most economical and least revolutionary adjustments which must be made in the system of rights and duties in response to only the most manifest and well-established changes, a lack of vigilance is almost indistinguishable from minding one's own business. To be more apprehensive would entail being less firm; and a greater readiness in government to reform the system of rights and duties would be inseparable from taking a larger command over the activities of the community. In short, in the absence of a larger enterprise, the sceptical office of keeping the system of rights and duties relevant to the current activities which compose the community may be expected to be sluggishly performed. Without the pull exerted by faith, without the 'perfectionism' which we have seen to be both an illusion and a dangerous illusion, itself evoking a nemesis, government in the sceptical style is liable to be overtaken by a nemesis of political quietism.

The disposition of scepticism to underestimate the occasion is another facet of this defeat. Faith recognizes every occasion as an emergency, and in the name of the 'public interest' or the 'public advantage' maintains its antinomian rule by calling upon the vast power at its command, which (because it is always insufficient) is always in process of being enlarged. The doctrine of 'eminent domain', for example, is magnified into a doctrine of 'sovereignty' and is understood not as an aid to the interpretation of the law, but as a law to end all laws, as authority for minute *ad hoc* control, as (in brief) the short-cut to heaven.[10]

In the sceptical style, on the other hand, for government to allow itself to be conditioned by emergency is already to be half-way to one manner of self-defeat. Strictly speaking, in this style, there can be no emergency: where law is at the mercy of occasion there is an end to the rule of law; and where modifications in the system of rights and duties are in response to extraordinary circumstances, they may introduce a temporary and local appropriateness but only at the cost of damaging the whole fabric which it is the office of government to protect.

Scepticism, therefore, is disposed to understatement. Rejecting the call of emergency in its own province, and being reluctant

---

[10] That in certain circumstances government may override private rights, including the rights of the subject against the government, is unavoidable; government, whatever its style, can consent to no absolute bar to its effectiveness. This doctrine is formulated in the concept of 'eminent domain', and it was understood to present no serious problems so long as government was turned in the direction of scepticism, that is so long as the 'circumstances' were narrowly rather than widely interpreted and the right exercised with diffidence. Indeed, that concept itself may be said to be sceptical because it distinguishes activity in an emergency from normal activity. But where the maximum begins to displace the minimum, where 'public necessity' is enlarged into 'well-being', 'prosperity' or 'salvation', or where any and every occasion may be designated an 'emergency' calling into operation the right of 'eminent domain', or where in some of its activities government always claims special privileges (e.g. the exclusion of specific performance from a contract) the right comes to swallow up all other rights, and from small beginnings a bastard and unmanageable doctrine of 'sovereignty' has appeared.

to go beyond its own province, it is liable to confuse a genuine emergency with the counterfeit emergencies of faith, and to discount it. But in doing so it displays an insufficiency which puts it on the road to the other manner of self-defeat to which it is liable. The energy and enterprise characteristic of modern European communities call for formality in government which the sceptical style can supply; but they call also for readiness in genuine emergency, and here this style is handicapped by its own virtues. The paradox of sceptical politics is that, while it is the style of government with the largest reserve of power available for use in emergency, it is also the least disposed to call upon this [reserve. It responds slowly to inspired imagining of perils to come. Yet the sceptical style cannot sustain itself as a purely empirical activity; it requires something more to attain coherence which, when it appears with unaccustomed passion and urgency, or as ideology, elicits a defensive response. Self-conscious dissatisfaction with the lack of projects designed to yield improving accomplishments overwhelms the habit of 'not doing'. Departure from studied self-limitation comes to seem unavoidable. In the presence of a style which is full of] passion and achieves its limited results by representing itself as a boundless enterprise, this studied self-limitation, this *mésure* on the part of government, must seem out of place, at best an oddity and at worst an example of indolence. It is always difficult to be enthusiastic about moderation or passionate about self-control, but in these circumstances it is impossible. Demanding neither love nor gratitude but only respect, this style of government will receive indifference or even contempt. While faith suffers the nemesis of excess, scepticism is deprived of its authority by its moderation.

Not to be readily understood by its subjects is, for a style of government, to be convicted of inappropriateness, even though the lack of understanding is a commentary on the subjects rather than on the style. And in this activist climate (in which the government of faith seems so preeminently relevant), the sceptical style must appear as an unintelligible piece of sophistication. Government in this style is, we have seen, primarily a judicial activity; and where men are intent upon achievement, either individual or communal, judicial activity is easily mistaken for a hindrance. It abdicates exactly at the point where the activist expects an assertion of authority; it withdraws where he expects it to proceed; it insists upon technicalities; it is narrow, severe and unenthusiastic; it is without courage or conviction. Here is a style of government which recognizes a multiplicity of directions of activity, and yet expresses approval of none; which assumes 'imperfection' and yet ventures upon no moral judgement. It sets a high value on precedent, but does not believe that the path of precedent leads to any specific destination.[11] It pretends to be determined by 'expediency' but in so refined a manner that it will not surrender itself to the pursuit of 'perfection'. In what seems a wanton self-limitation, it refuses to defend a man in such a manner as to deprive him of all authority to defend himself. If the activist is concerned with 'truth', a law of evidence which precludes a court from hearing what, if heard, would establish guilt, appears an obstructive technicality. If he is concerned with 'good husbandry', to allow proprietary rights to stand in the way is absurd. If he is concerned with 'righteousness', to make peace with the 'heathen' is vile. In short, the intellectual distinctions which constitute this style of government are foreign to the activist climate of opinion; in a world where all other activities are serious, where diligence is virtue and energy excellence, they fix upon government the character of frivolity.

No doubt this judgement of the politics of scepticism suffers from both ignorance and misconception. Nevertheless, it reveals a certain inappropriateness in the style, and, what is more important, it leads us, if we will allow it to do so, to the final nemesis of scepticism: the disposition to reduce politics to play.

By 'play',[12] I mean activity pursued on certain specified occasions, at fixed times and in a place set apart and according to exact rules, the significance of the activity lying not in a terminal result aimed at, but in the disposition which is enjoyed and fostered in the cause of the activity. This manner of activity is contrasted, in general, with 'serious' activity or with what may be called 'ordinary life'. Without 'earnest' there can be no 'play'; without 'play' there can be no 'earnest'. Consequently, 'play' is not merely or directly opposed to 'serious' activity; its relationship to 'ordinary life' is that of an ironical companion. It exhibits

---

[11] 'Precisely because I believe that the world would be just as well off if it lived under laws different from ours in many ways, and because I believe that the claim of our special code to respect is simply that it exists, that it is the one to which we have become accustomed and not that it represents an eternal principle, I am slow to consent to overruling a precedent, and think that our important duty is to see that the judicial duel shall be fought out in its accustomed way.' Holmes, *Collected Legal Papers*, p. 239.

[12] See J. Huizinga, *Homo Ludens*.

in itself the tensions, the violence and the 'seriousness' of 'ordinary life', but they are a mockery of their originals and when reflected back upon 'ordinary life' they have the effect of deflating its 'seriousness' by reducing the significance of the ends pursued.

There is, of course, a 'playful' component in most of our activities: in business and in religion. And whenever we insist upon the manner rather than the result we are, in this sense, 'at play'. But nowhere is this component more clearly present than in the various levels of political activity, in the conduct of affairs at home, in the administration of justice, in diplomacy and in war. How large and how significant a place 'play' is recognized to have will, of course, depend upon our interpretation of the detail of these activities, but on any interpretation this component is conspicuous both in the administration of justice and in the conduct of parliamentary government. For both these activities there is a place and time set apart, marking them off from the world outside. The persons engaged in these activities play a part which distinguishes their behaviour, there and then, from what it is elsewhere: their movements conform to a ritual and their manner of speech is guarded by special privileges and determined by exact rules. Friends appear as opponents; there is dispute without hatred, conflict without violence; victory is subordinated to accepted rules and conventions; to win a point by the ingenious exploitation of procedure is recognized to be legitimate, but failure to observe the ritual (even though it is inadvertent failure) disqualifies the contestant; and the whole is enveloped in a convention which allows victory by words and in no other manner.

In all this there is much that is foreign to the politics of faith. This style of government is preeminently 'serious'. Political activity is approximated to 'ordinary life', and the terminal result is held to be more important than the manner in which it is achieved. Debate is argument, not conversation; and when the direction of activity has been determined, 'opposition' has no place. Indeed, all the features of modern European government which we have already observed to be regrettable from the standpoint of faith are those which belong to the component of 'playfulness'; and whenever our politics has turned decisively in the direction of faith, it is this component which has been reduced or suppressed. On the other hand, it is the component of 'play' which preeminently represents scepticism: indeed, it may be identified with the sceptical style. Political activity is recognized as a limited activity, distinguished from 'ordinary life'. The insistence upon formality in the conduct of affairs; the terminal result subordinated to the manner of its achievement; the understanding of debate as conversation and as a perpetual partner in the activity of governing; the recognition of devices (such as majority decisions) as nothing more than convenient conventions; the understanding of the limited significance of victory – all these are at once characteristic of the politics of scepticism and of politics as 'play'. And the sceptic would go on to observe that the relationship between government in this style and the activities of its subjects is, in many respects, the relationship between 'play' and 'ordinary life'. To govern is not the 'serious' business of setting activity in a certain direction and supplying it with energy and an object; it is providing current activities with a ready and continuously appropriate means of resolving the difficulties generated by their passionate and exclusive concentration upon themselves, and in this manner lessening the violence of the impact of one activity upon another. That this cannot be done without an endowment of power is obvious. But the sceptic will remark that the necessary power is small and that the manner in which it is exercised, its formality and moderation, is itself an ironical criticism of the excess and self-centredness of the activities it controls.

The poles of our politics may, then, be reformulated as 'earnest' and 'play'. And 'earnest' and 'play' are both opponents and partners, so faith and scepticism are both enemies and friends. Scepticism represents the extreme of 'play', and its nemesis (when it stands alone, deprived of the modifying pull of 'earnest') will be that which belongs to the character of 'play'.

There is a certain extemporizing exuberance which is apt to appear within the exactness which belongs to 'play': a disposition to overdo things. But this is not the forerunner of collapse; it is merely a manifestation of the latitude which an exact outline permits; it is the *play* within 'play'. When, however, the passion to win supervenes, the spell is broken and 'play' is at an end. Nevertheless, though this is defeat, it is not self-defeat. The self-defeat of 'play' is the lethargy which overtake the game when one of the players is wholly indifferent about winning. We give away points because we see it pleases our opponent to win; but all to no purpose. The apathy communicates itself, the 'play' goes to pieces and the game collapses. In 'play', properly speaking, victory and defeat are irrelevant; but without the illusion that winning matters, 'play' is impossible. This is the nemesis of 'play': the belief that there is *nothing* serious in mortality. But, just as the irony of scepticism can recall faith from the self-defeat that belongs to its uninhibited character, so the pull of faith, the illusion that there is a victory to be won (and not a resort to the extreme of faith), rescues from self-destruction a style of politics disposed to reduce the activity of governing to mere 'play'.[13]

IV

To say that each of these styles of government, when it stands by itself, is self-destructive, and to say that what can rescue each from self-destruction is something that the other is able to supply, is perhaps only a picturesque way of saying that faith and scepticism in modern European politics are not merely opponents, but also partners. Our enquiry into the nemesis of each of these styles no more than reinforces the view that they are not, properly speaking, alternative manners of governing and understandings of the office of government but the poles of the internal movement of our politics.

But it has brought to light a characteristic of faith and scepticism which has hitherto been noticeable but not properly noticed, namely, the fact that these two styles do not exactly match one another. They oppose one another, but the opposition is oblique; they are partners, but they do not enjoy exactly the same standing. It is only when we consider the respective inabilities of faith and scepticism to stand alone that this inequality declares itself unmistakably.

Self-defeat is a necessary characteristic of the politics of faith. I do not mean that, in the long run, the pursuit of this style of government is bound to land a community, especially a community of the kind that exists in modern Europe, in destruction; this may be so, but it is not the point. I mean that this style of government is inherently self-contradictory. On the other hand, the politics of scepticism suffers only from a strong contingent liability to self-defeat: when it stands alone it stands unsteadily. Consequently, while the pull of scepticism may rescue faith from certain self-destruction, the pull of faith saves scepticism from only probable self-destruction.

---

[13] cf. Shaftesbury, *Characteristicks* (2nd edn), vol. I, p. 74.

If the politics of scepticism represented mere anarchy, then this style of government would be inherently self-contradictory, and would be as fully dependent upon faith as in fact faith is upon it: anarchy and faith, when they stand alone, are each, in different manners, the abolition of 'government'. But scepticism is not anarchy; it is not even disposed to anarchy. And in virtue of its escape from anarchy, it escapes inherent self-destruction as a manner of government. The defects of its virtues are serious, and if they were fully operative it would certainly be no better than a limping style of politics, but it is not necessary that they should be fully operative. For the most part, the inappropriateness of the sceptical style to the communities of modern Europe (which is its greatest defeat) is an inappropriateness to a condition which it does not itself promote, namely, a condition of 'emergency' and 'war'. It is true that 'war' is to be considered a normal rather than an abnormal condition of modern European communities, but this is not (so far as major conflict is concerned) a consequence of the character of the communities themselves, but of their political activity having been turned frequently and for long periods in the aggressive direction of faith. The major conflicts of modern times have either been religious, or a product of the pursuit of 'perfection' understood as the maximum exploitation of the resources of the world, or in defence of 'perfection' as 'security'. A manner of government unready to recognize and unsuited to meet this condition may be said to be likely to suffer defeat when it appears, and may be said to be inappropriate if the chances are that it will appear, but it does nothing to encourage the appearance.

And further, the excess, the absence of self-limitation, which belongs to the style of faith when it stands alone is both characteristic and always complete in the sense that it is always as great as the power available permits it to be; but, since scepticism in politics is not anarchy, the severe self-limitation that is characteristic of it (and in virtue of which it is both a 'moral' activity and a vulnerable activity) is not an extreme; it does not limit itself out of existence. The style of faith, when it stands alone, is not susceptible of degrees, there is no more or less, it is always at the end of its tether and is incapable of the kind of self-criticism which would enable it to defend itself against its own excesses. It is, as we have seen, the politics of immortality, building for eternity. But the sceptical style, even when it stands alone, is capable of some self-criticism; there is a recognized limit to which it can compare its achievements, and ·it enjoys some reserve and scope for internal movement and self-correction. It is the politics of mortality, which does not mean that the range of its vision is confined to a present instant, but that it is neither short nor long. Everything in this style of government is provisional and is constructed so that it may be enlarged or diminished as unfolding circumstances demand; but there are degrees of evanescence, and what is transitory is, on that account, not merely momentary. Government in the style of faith is a godlike activity; in the style of scepticism it is a human activity, not the activity of a day-fly. In short, if we regard these poles of our political activity as positive and negative, it is necessary to recognize that while the style of faith stands for 'everything', the complete control of the activities which compose a community, the style of scepticism stands, not for 'nothing', but for 'little'.

Moreover, this inequality between the characters of faith and scepticism may be formulated in a general practical principle: excess and defect are not equidistant from the mean. As Isocrates observed, and Confucius before him, 'moderation lies in deficiency rather than in excess':[14] indeed, deficiency itself enjoys a mean because it is never absolute. The spendthrift may dispose of all and rather more than all that he possesses, but even the miser must spend something; the marksman whose first bullet falls short may see where it falls and may dispose himself accordingly to hit the mark next time, but he whose first bullet wings its way into a distance where the eye cannot follow it is no nearer to hitting the mark than if he had never fired. And whatever may be the limitations of this principle, I think we may find it useful when we come to consider what conclusions it is permissible to draw from this understanding of our politics.

---

[14] Isocrates, *Ad Nicoclem*, p. 33; Confucius, *Analects*, iv. p. 23.

6

CONCLUSION

I

Human activity, with whatever it may be concerned, enjoys a circumscribed range of movement. The limits which define this range are historic, that is to say, they are themselves the product of human activity. Generally speaking, there are no 'natural' limits as distinct from historic limits: those which we ascribe to 'human nature', for example, are not less historic than those which we immediately recognize as springing from conditions determined by human activity. Even what a man may do with his physical strength is determined by the historic devices and inventions of men, and no community has been without such devices. Being historic, they are not absolute, but on any occasion they are not on that account any the less limits. They may be wide or narrow, they are never absent. The flight of imagination, the poet's power over words and images, the scientist's hypotheses, the philosopher's engagements and disengagements and the practical man's projects and enterprises are all of them exploitations of what is given or intimated in the condition of the world he inhabits. And, from one point of view, civilization is distinguished from barbarism in respect of at once greater latitude and firmer limits for the play of activity.

So it is with our political activity, the understanding and care of public arrangements. The politician has always a certain field of vision and a certain range of opportunity; what he is able to contemplate, to desire or to attempt is subject to the historic limits of this situation. And in order to understand his activity it is necessary first to consider the field within which he moves, the choices that are available to him and the enterprises he is able to entertain. Indeed, until we have understood this, any other judgement we may make about his activity – judgements of approval or disapproval, for example – are liable to lack force and relevance. The limits of this field, like those of any other, are not, of course, fixed for all time; they are historic and therefore always on the move, contracting and expanding. Nevertheless, on any occasion they are relatively fixed, and the contraction and expansion themselves are never fortuitous or without limit, but are always the exploitation of intimations. The most free politician is one whose profound knowledge both of the opportunities and the limits of his historic situation makes readily available to him not merely a few of its intimations, but the whole range of its possibilities, and at the same time does not provoke him to enterprises which are without foundation in his circumstances.

Political activity in the conditions of modern Europe is movement within a certain field of historic possibilities. During this half-millennium these possibilities have expanded in some directions and contracted in others: what may be contemplated now is in some respects a smaller and in others a larger range of activity than it was five hundred years ago. But these contractions and expansions are relatively insignificant. The range of internal movement is fundamentally unchanged: modern history may be said to have been inaugurated by a peculiarly large and rapid expansion of political possibilities, and its course, from this point of view, has been the more and more thorough exploitation of a range of movement then opened up. To understand the politics of modern Europe, then, is, in the first place, to recognize their characteristic range of movement. In other words, political activity in modern Europe is the exploitation of the dispositions which belong to the political 'character' of modern Europe – a character distinguished by a certain range of internal movement.

The two dispositions, into which the impulses of the modern European political character have come to group themselves, I have called respectively the politics of faith and the politics of scepticism. From one point of view these are two 'ideal' understandings and styles of government opposed to one another, not directly but obliquely. And the politics of modern Europe have more often been disposed in one or other of these directions than they have come to rest at one or other of these horizons. Nevertheless, from this point of view, the politics of faith and the politics of scepticism are exclusive styles of governing, and the pursuits of government in modern times have been a *concordia discors* of these two styles.

But they are not merely two opposed styles of politics, nor are they merely the extremes of which our political character is capable, inert barriers which it may from time to time encounter and which it is unable to pass. They are, more properly, the 'charges' of the poles of our political activity, each exerting a pull which makes itself felt over the whole range of movement. And our political activity has been at all times, even when it has moved far in one or other of these directions, the resultant of both these pulls and not merely the consequence of one. Hence the politics of faith and the politics of scepticism are not, properly speaking, alternative styles of government; they provide at once the limits and the impetus of our political movement. And the characteristic range of movement is conditioned by these extremes in a way in which it would not be if they were merely its boundaries. Moreover, this polarity has given to our political activity its peculiar ambivalence, and to our political vocabulary its characteristic ambiguity. If there were no opportunity of internal movement, there would be no ambiguity; and if the internal movement were governed by other extremes, then the ambiguity would be different from what it is.

This, then, is the nature of political movement in modern Europe, and these are the limits which both contain and inspire it: this is our predicament. It remains now to consider what conclusions may be drawn from this view of our political situation. And in particular to consider whether there is not a proper manner of being active for this particular political character.

II

Our first impulse, no doubt, will be to conclude that, whatever the practical usefulness of ambivalence and ambiguity, we should be much better off if this complex manner of politics were reduced to simplicity. Whatever we lost in richness and variety, we should recover in the absence of distraction: it is as foolish to expect complexity without ambiguity as to expect that fire will warm but not burn. And the imposition of simplicity upon our political character would have the virtue of depriving politics of the exaggerated importance that they have come to enjoy: they are believed to be important largely because they are difficult, and they are difficult largely because they are complicated. This enterprise has long been attractive to the bolder (and, perhaps, the more impatient) spirits, who early came to see it as the only sure manner of correcting the confusion of modern European politics. 'Lo, what disorder!' exclaims one of the seventeenth-century representatives of this view;[1] and as the panorama of chaos unrolls itself before him, he has a vision of the symmetry which might replace it. Moreover, more recent admirers of a simple style of politics may point to the success that has attended similar projects in other fields. The complexity characteristic of our law (the consequence of its heterogeneous pedigree and an absence of the courage necessary to discard from time to time what could be recognized only as encumbrances) has been notably reduced during the last hundred and fifty years. But, in the main, the victories of the simplifiers of our law have been in the province of procedure, and while there may be both room and opportunity for reducing the complexity of our political procedures, this scarcely touches the significant complexity of our politics. The enterprise of the reformers of the law is analogous to that of simplifying our spelling, whereas the project of a simple politics is analogous, in the magnitude of the undertaking, to simplifying a language: the restriction of vocabulary and syntax such as belongs, for example, to 'basic English', or (on another plane) the creation of our 'English' language from which all Latinisms have been excluded. This, indeed, is the kind of simple politics which the physiocrat had in mind who conjectured that 'it would suffice to have that amount of capacity and patience which a child good at arithmetic employs, in order to become a good politician and a truly good citizen'.[2]

The enterprise, then, of removing the ambiguity of our politics by abolishing their complexity is not to be undertaken without first determining the simple pattern to be imposed. The simplification of procedure may be achieved merely by the removal of some of the accretions of time which have become meaningless or obstructive, or by the exclusion of conspicuous anomalies, but a simple style of politics calls for a more radical kind of reform. And unless our inventor comes forward with an entirely new style of politics, an artifice analogous to a new language with a vocabulary and a syntax of its own, the choice

[1] Comenius, *The Labyrinth of the World.*

[2] Georges Weulersse, *Le Mouvement physiocratique en France de 1756 à 1770*, ii, p. 123.

before us is between one or other of the styles which at present distract us. And there is no doubt that the selection of one and the exclusion of the other would eliminate the ambiguity of our political vocabulary. This, indeed, is the character of all the concrete proposals for removing complexity from European politics. Marxism, for example, is a simple-minded project of this kind: it bids us forsake all manners of political activity save that which is appropriate to a certain version, the Baconian version, of the politics of faith. The enterprise of communism is to simplify not merely political activity, but all activity whatsoever; all problems are reduced to one problem. And it is perhaps the only plan for the simplification of European politics in which the inappropriateness of a simple style of politics to a complex society is clearly perceived. It is the ideal model of all simple styles of politics, and its pedigree may be traced back to the early projects of escape from complexity in the seventeenth and eighteenth centuries.

Nevertheless, our reading of modern European politics suggests conclusive reasons for believing that a simple style of politics is not merely inappropriate to the character of modern European communities but is inherently self-defeating: it is an escape from the consequences of complexity which leads nowhere. If our choice lies (as it does) between one of the two current styles which compose our complex manner of political activity, then it is Hobson's choice: in selecting either we are requiring of it something which it cannot supply. For, as we have seen, the politics of faith and the politics of scepticism are not alternative styles of politics, but the 'charges' of the two poles between which modern European politics moves and has moved for near five hundred years. Each, in the abstract, may have the virtue of simplicity; but neither, as we know them, is capable of being by itself a concrete style of political activity. And we have observed what the character of each would be if its partnership with the other were dissolved. Faith would simplify politics by abolishing them; and the vices of a scepticism unqualified by the pull of faith may be expected shortly to overwhelm it. It may be concluded, then, that we cannot escape from our predicament by imposing simplicity upon our politics: there is no intimation in our situation of any but a complex manner of political activity. Our task is to find some means of being at home in the complexity we have inherited, and cannot now avoid, without indulging ourselves in the false hope of discovering a market in which we can exchange it for simplicity.

III

The character of our politics being what it is – unavoidably complex – we must learn to exploit its virtues. And there can be no doubt that its virtues may be most fully enjoyed and its vices most certainly avoided while we hold back from the extremes of which it is capable and explore the central area which lies between. Indeed, the preeminent characteristic of a complex style of politics is its offer of a habitable middle region in which we may escape the self-destructive extremes. To be at home in this style, then, is to observe what may be called the mean in action.[3] Its principle is: *il faut jamais outré*. Nor is this an extraneous principle, imposed from the outside by some arbitrary belief that virtue everywhere is a mean between extremes. This belief may be true; but here the mean is a principle which a complex style of politics itself divulges; if our politics were not complex, if they pointed unmistakably in one direction only, then this principle would be absurd. And further, in so far as we recognize modern European politics for what they are, and do not deny one half of their character, their operation can be seen to be disposed towards the occupation of this middle region; we leave it only when one or other of the poles of our politics fails to exert its pull. The principle of the mean, then, is inherent in a complex manner of politics, and it is rescued here from platitude by our having before us a clear notion of the specific extremes concerned. Moreover, it must be observed that the mean here is not a fixed point; the principle of the mean in action does not deprive our politics of internal movement or impose simplicity upon them. A complex style of politics can be immobilized only when it ceases to be complex by coming to rest at one of its horizons; the mean is a middle region of movement, not a central point of repose.

There is a passage in the fortunes of our politics, appearing appropriately at a time when they were disposed to run from one extreme to the other, in the late seventeenth and early eighteenth century, in which this principle of the mean in action first fully emerged. It is a passage which has none of the glamour of politics run to an extreme or of causes passionately embraced,

---

[3] I take this expression from the Confucian philosopher Tzu Szu, who, appropriately for my purpose, contrasts it not only with excess in action, but also with the absolutism of 'knowledge'.

but it reveals the concrete character of a complex manner of politics more unmistakably than any of the more spectacular occasions. It did not appear for want of passion on either side, nor was it an example of politics merely in the doldrums. Enthusiasm was not so much decried as put in its proper place.

Faith had knocked up an impressive score, and its innings ended characteristically in hit-wicket. (The scorers, unaware of what had happened, went on chalking up the runs: faith, particularly in France, was believed to have 'a splendid future behind it'.) In the situation, however, it looked as if scepticism would take a mighty revenge. But not at all; the contest was adjourned for tea. And in the conversation that ensued, the political principle of the mean in action made its appearance. Many voices were heard in this conversation, but among the more notable participants were Locke, Berkeley, Shaftesbury, Halifax, Boyle, St Evremond, Fontenelle and Hume, and there were wits (like de Mandeville) on the circumference who provided the comedy. They did not compose a political party; they did not belong to a single nation, nor were they the first to perceive the character of modern politics; they drew largely upon the thoughts of others who had gone before, and their view was naturally limited by their immediate situation. The conversation was not confined to politics, but ranged over the whole field of human conduct. This was unfortunate, because the precise political principle of the mean in action was obscured in a general deprecation of excess and 'enthusiasm' and a general advocacy of 'moderation' and 'good humour' in all human relations. Political activity, the care of the public arrangements of a community, was hardly perceived as a specific kind of activity, and the principle of moderation, which should have been detected in the character of modern politics, appeared as if it were a political principle because it was, in the first place, a general principle of human conduct. However, in spite of this confusion, the notion of the mean in political activity was not lost. A suggestion of it had appeared in the English Act of Indemnity and Oblivion of 1660, with its plea that the nation should be brought back to 'its old good humour'; but it came to little. It was expounded, however, with notable skill in Halifax's *The Character of a Trimmer*, though this did not stand alone; it was one of many attempts to elicit the principle of 'moderation' from the conditions of modern politics, and the 'trimmer', of course, existed as a man before he became a 'character'.

Halifax was a political sceptic and so also, in different degrees, were his companions in this enterprise. But it is not remarkable that it should be sceptics who first uncovered the principle of the mean in modern politics. For although the sceptical style is itself an extreme, its extremity is not to impose a single pattern of activity upon a community, and consequently it enjoys (as we have seen) a characteristic forbearance of its own which can be seen to intimate a wider doctrine of moderation. Nevertheless, what Halifax offers us in *The Character of a Trimmer* is not a doctrine of scepticism, but a doctrine of moderation. And here his only handicap was his imperfect perception of the essential polarity of modern politics which sprang from his concern with the peculiarities of the current situation: the extremes between which his mean lies are 'authority' (or 'monarchy') and 'liberty' (or 'commonwealth'), and these, on account of their ambiguity and local reference, are not the genuine horizons of modern politics and stand to one side of faith and scepticism.

The principle of the mean in action is, then, the virtue of exploiting the middle range of our political opportunities, the faculty of not taking the words of our political vocabulary in their utmost extent. The 'trimmer' is one who disposes his weight so as to keep the ship upon an even keel. And our inspection of his conduct reveals certain general ideas at work. He is concerned only with the internal movement of politics; his notion (as Halifax says) is merely that 'it would do as well, if the Boat went even'. This is not because he necessarily shares the sceptic's doubt whether there is any movement except internal, but because he believes that such other movement as there may turn out to be must be left to take care of itself: to recognize 'progressive' movement as the direct concern of government is to have embraced the politics of faith. Being concerned to prevent politics from running to extremes, he believes that there is a time for everything and that everything has its time – not providentially, but empirically. He will be found facing in whatever direction the occasion seems to require if the boat is to go even. Nevertheless, his changes of direction will neither be frequent, sudden nor great; for the changes his movement is designed to counterbalance are not, for the most part, either frequent or sudden. Further, he will recognize the necessity of others facing in a different direction from himself: the mean in action is never to be achieved by a general surge this way or that; indeed, such surges are precisely what it is designed to exclude. A small movement, if it is timely, will be less disconcerting than a large one at a later stage. And he may consider that the course of modern politics allows of some rough generalizations. For example, he may expect to find the young more sensitive to one kind of intimation in our politics and to turn naturally in the direction of faith, and the older to recognize more readily other intimations and to have an affinity with the prudent diffidence of scepticism. In this manner he will understand the different groups and sections in his community in respect of their natural and historic dispositions, regarding none as incapable of making a contribution.[4] Neither Dionysus nor Apollo, but each in his place and season. Or again, he will think it probable that a relatively simple community will be more easily overwhelmed by the prospects which the style of faith seems to offer than one which enjoys a confident and well-established variety of directions of activity, and he will dispose his expectations and his weight accordingly. Success he will observe with suspicion, and he will lend his support more readily to weakness than to power; he will dissent without dissidence, and approve without irrevocably committing himself. In opposition he will not deny the value of what he opposes, only its appropriateness; and his support carries with it only the judgement that what is supported is opportune.

The 'trimmer', then, this political character which belongs to a complex manner of political activity, is a 'time-server'. He has a closer affinity to scepticism than to faith, and he has the advantage of the sceptic in his ability to recognize change and emergency. His needs are knowledge and judgement: knowledge of the polarity of the politics within which he moves, and judgement to recognize the proper occasions and directions of movement. And if there is anything to be added about his character, it is this: that his natural home is not necessarily in a middle party. Centre parties often take credit for moderation, but as often as not it is a spurious moderation which has nothing to do with the mean in action. Exerting their power to hold a balance between the current party extremities, which are not to

---

[4] To Pascal, who came to observe this principle in respect of the poles represented by the Jesuits and the Jansenists in his day, it appeared as a duty of 'professing two opposite truths'. And although he recognized that the situation called upon him to support one rather than the other, in the end he suffered the revulsion which comes to any honest man when he finds himself pushed to an extreme which he does not wish to occupy. *Pensées*, p. 865; cp. Montaigne, *Essais*, III. p. xi.

be expected to correspond with the essential horizons of our politics, they usually enjoy less self-command than the extremities themselves.

In a word, the politics of the mean in action is appropriateness. There will be minor and subsidiary polarities which on occasion attract our attention and govern our conduct;[5] but, in the end, appropriateness is to be judged in relation to what has become the principal polarity of our politics: for the politics of modern Europe the relevant horizons are faith and scepticism.

IV

If this account of things has any merit, it is as a guide for political reasoning: it offers us a manner of thinking about our politics. Its limitations are obvious: it does not provide mistake-proof answers to any of the questions that appear when we think about politics, and there are some questions which require a different (or a narrower) setting if they are to be formulated in a manner to be answerable. But it does supply a frame within which to set our thoughts to work. It allows us to get some of the more important questions in order, and it gives us a preview of the shape an answer must have if it is to be a relevant conclusion. Moreover, the help this manner of reasoning provides even when what we are considering are day-to-day movements in politics is not negligible. Indeed, my contention is that if a politician needs more than a charitable disposition, a fund of common sense to draw upon and imagination to forecast the moves of his opponents, what he needs is neither a doctrine which will give him infallible solutions to his problems, nor a merely general idea of what political activity is about, but something between the two: a view of his situation, of its limits and possibilities, such as we have been investigating. In default of this we are without any sense of political direction, and the exchange of political opinions will remain as unprofitable as it usually is.

On this view of our political predicament, how shall we read our present situation, and what conclusions does it encourage? I suppose the most obvious conclusion which springs from this

---

[5] Halifax, Burke and de Tocqueville are notable examples of the pursuit of this principle in respect of the local and subsidiary.

manner of thinking about what is afoot is that the politics of faith is in the ascendant. The invitation to power has proved irresistible; the lust of government has overwhelmed us. If it were merely the case that the governments and parties everywhere in power had their eyes turned in the direction of this extreme, it would be a considerable exaggeration to say that the politics of faith had established itself as the favoured style. The ground of this observation is that no regime can now expect to remain in power, and no party can expect to be listened to, which does not at least have the appearance of looking in this direction. The programme of every party is written in the language of faith, the enterprise of every government is conceived in the idiom of faith. And the most notable political gift of Europe to the world is not representative institutions or 'popular' government, or indeed any form of government at all, but the ambition and inspiration to govern and be governed in the manner of faith. Nor is this a sudden or very recent turn of affairs: the seventeenth century had its adventures in this direction, and the tide has been setting in this direction for at least a hundred and fifty years.

There are some observers who take this as a sign of providential approval for this style; or if they do not attribute the ascendancy of the politics of faith to the blessing of God or the grace of History, they find in it evidence of the inherent merit of the politics of faith or of its peculiar appropriateness to the contemporary situation. That it has some appropriateness to some part of our situation is, of course, unavoidable; to the extent which the situation has itself come to be conditioned by the ascendancy of this style of government, it must be expected to have that much appropriateness. Nevertheless, it is clear that this belief in the unmitigated beneficence of the politics of faith belongs to some other manner of political reasoning than that which I have been pursuing. It is enough to remind ourselves of the generation, character and 'form' of this style of government in order to perceive that the punters who have made it the favourite have sadly misjudged it. The pedigree, by Power out of Fond Hope is not reasoning; gross stamina allied to mere speed, oddly enough, never got a satisfactory animal. No doubt there are courses over which it will win a small race or two, no doubt there are conditions which favour its chances; it is capable of getting away to a good start, it shows a fair turn of speed over about three furlongs, and it acts well downhill. But in the long run this milk-cart Derby candidate is destined to disappoint.

The political activity of modern Europe, in the view I have taken of it, is a movement between two poles, and the politics of faith is merely the 'charge' of one of these poles. It is an extreme style of government which, when it stands alone, is self-destructive. And the more decisively our political activity is drawn towards this extreme, the more fully it partakes of the self-defeat. Moreover, if we remain unconvinced by the evidence of incapacity which a mere analysis of its character affords, it is impossible to remain unmoved by the character which the current ascendancy of faith has given to our politics. When we consider this impulse to 'perfection' which has become the principal guide for European political activity, the sublime confidence that it is hurrying us away from an ignorant past now happily in ruins, the faith that significant history is the story of the operation of this impulse and that everything that impedes it is evil and is in process of being cancelled out for ever; when we consider how the faithful servants of this impulse, intoxicated at having been dealt four aces, at once staked the maximum and thought it mattered nothing how they played the hand; when we consider how hopefully nation after nation has set out in this direction, its attention fixed upon what might be harvested on the way and heedless of the nemesis which waited at the end; and when we consider that all this is built upon nothing morally more substantial than the power that made it possible – we may perhaps wonder whether we ought not to regard it as a piece of somnabulism, an aberration rather than a pilgrimage.

But that is not exactly the view of it suggested by the manner of political reasoning we are pursuing. This passage in the history of our politics is neither a mere aberration, nor is it (what it takes itself to be) a final orientation of our political activity: it is a flight to one of the extremes of which our complex politics is capable. In it, all the defects of this extreme have revealed themselves unmistakably. Earlier adventures in this direction, because they were impelled by less extensive power and held in check by a more lively scepticism, merely intimated what has now appeared. Consequently, mere denunciation is out of place. We have to recognize it, not in its own terms as a final simplification of our politics, but as the exclusive pursuit of one of their potentialities. And *not* to pursue it is neither to be 'reactionary' nor to be self-convicted of treason.

In a complex manner of politics it is above all appropriate for political activity to retain its freedom of movement by perpetually recalling itself from whatever extreme threatens to overwhelm it. The man who has this in the forefront of his understanding I have called a 'trimmer'. And his task in the current situation is clear. It is, first, to restore the understanding of the complexity of modern politics. In the present circumstances this is, perhaps, his most difficult task: the ascendancy of faith has obscured, indeed almost obliterated, this understanding by imposing upon our politics a counterfeit simplicity. Secondly, his task is to renew the vitality of political scepticism so that this pole of our politics can once more exert its pull. Thirdly, in his participation in politics, he must dispose his weight against the prevailing current – not in order to make it flow to the opposite extreme, but to recall our political activity to that middle region of movement in which it is sensitive to the pull of both its poles and immobilizes itself at neither of its extremes. And he may do this with confidence, because the current he opposes is sanctified neither by God or History; its direction is neither inevitable nor profitable. But here, once more, it is necessary to observe that this third task is one for which there is scope within every one of the political parties and alignments of modern European politics, all of which are now deeply conditioned by the ascendancy of the politics of faith, though of course some much more so than others. Precisely what movements the 'trimmer' is called upon to make will depend upon the exact position in which he finds himself, but, for the present, wherever he is he will make himself known as the partizan of scepticism and will recognize the partizans of power (wherever they appear) as his proper opponents.

If these tasks could be performed only by calling into existence habits of conduct hitherto unknown, and ideas hitherto foreign to our politics, they would compose a pointless and profitless enterprise; indeed, this would be only another way of saying that government in the style of faith is the sole intimation of our manner of politics. But this is not so. However far out of sight the complexity of our politics may have fallen, it has never been obliterated. And in this respect the task of the 'trimmer' is to rescue our political activity from gross misconception. There are, in fact, still abundant resources, uncorrupted by the ascendancy of faith, which the 'trimmer' in his present situation may call upon. Unfortunately, the version of English parliamentary government which has been spread around the world is the bastard progeny of faith ('popular government' in the service of perfection), but there remains in that service of government the resources of a still undiminished scepticism. And while the writers who belong to the great sceptical tradition (not all of them, of course, unabated sceptics) – Augustine, Pascal, Hobbes, Locke, Halifax, Hume, Burke, Paine, Bentham, Coleridge, Burckhardt, de Tocqueville, Acton – though for a season they have been displaced in popular favour by the pundits of faith, wait only to be recalled and reinterpreted. None of these, perhaps, is able to speak directly to this generation, but in this respect they are better placed than the apostles of faith, who for two centuries have merely repeated themselves. And, in my opinion, there is no better starting place for a renewed attempt to understand and to modernize the principles of the sceptical tradition in our politics than a study of Pascal and Hume.

V

It remains to consider what this view of things, this manner of political reasoning, contributes to our understanding and management of the ambiguity of our political vocabulary.

In any reading of the politics of modern Europe the ambiguity of political language is sufficiently remarkable to call for investigation, and in our reading it appears as the emblem of what is most characteristic in this passage in our politics: it is a reflection of ambivalence in our political pursuits. Hence, it is to be understood neither as an invention of the devil to make us see double and mistake our allegiance, nor as a sign of defeat or failure, nor again as merely a careless or disingenuous corruption of the proper meanings of words. On the contrary, it is intrinsic in our politics and affords one of the most convincing pieces of evidence that the politics of modern Europe are complex and not simple: if they intimated a single direction of movement, if in fact they were already immobilized or were in process of becoming stuck at one of their horizons and had no middle range of movement, then (and on that account) our vocabulary would be unequivocal. Moreover, this reading of our politics, in revealing the historic extremes which limit and govern the accepted directions of movement in modern European politics, reveals also the precise character of the principal ambiguity of our language. It is because we are distracted between these particular directions of activity that the words in our political vocabulary have come to possess their particular range of meaning and so to be ambiguous in this particular way.

The first conclusion that suggests itself is that we may abolish this ambiguity only by imposing upon our politics a simple character (a single direction of attention) which they do not at present possess. But, since the available simplicities are what they are, to impose a simple character is not only impossible but is indistinguishable from self-defeat. In some circumstances a single manner of politics may exist and be appropriate; but in our circumstances it involves the immobilization of our politics at one of their extremes, neither of which is capable, by itself, of supplying a concrete manner of political activity. In short, the enterprise of merely removing the ambiguity of the political vocabulary of modern Europe is chimerical.

But our reading of modern politics leaves us with something more than this negative conclusion. It calls our attention to the practical benefits of this ambiguity: its power to modify the violence of the extremes in our politics and to mediate them to one another. There are, of course, dangers in the exploitation of this benefit, but it offers an opportunity which will be despised only by those, certain of the propriety of pursuing 'perfection' and certain of the direction in which it lies, who are careless of everything on the way: the politics of faith alone regards ambiguity as worthless. But to be at home in a complex manner of politics and to know how to manage it is to be able to enjoy the practical benefits of ambiguity without allowing it to generate intellectual confusion. If political activity were argument designed to elucidate or to 'prove' the truth of propositions, this would be difficult; but in modern Europe this is not so. Politics is a conversation between diverse interests, in which activities that circumstantially limit one another are saved from violent collision; and here, words which have within them a little latitude of meaning (words, indeed, which have a continuous range of meaning in which the extreme meanings are mediated to one another) may sometimes serve our turn better than a scientific vocabulary designed to exclude all doubleness.

Nevertheless, this manner of understanding modern politics does not merely applaud the ambiguity of our political language, and it does not leave it entirely untouched. To have perceived the ground and the range of the ambiguity is to have deprived it of some of its power to confuse. Moreover, it puts us in a position to recognize the significant differences and disparities, and to observe the significant affinities.

Consider, for example, the word 'democracy'. It is a manifold word, referring to two different sets of ideas. It stands for a certain view of the authorization or constitution of government: it is an answer to the problem of the 'tenure of magistrates'; it means a manner of collecting the power to be at the disposal of government and a manner of controlling the activity of governing. And in this respect it is connected with various 'institutions', styled 'popular', such as elected parliaments and accountable ministers. But, in common parlance, the word means something else as well: it stands for the activity of governing turned in a certain direction. And here it may mean either government turned in the direction of faith, or government turned in the direction of scepticism: both the current styles of governing have appropriated the word. And they are able to do so because the 'popular' institutions connected with a so-called 'democratic' authorization of government are eligible for interpretation in either of these directions. Nevertheless, it is clear that what is significant in the first place is the manner of governing, because it is this which determines how the authorization or constitution of government is understood. If the manner is that of faith, then 'institutions' are understood solely in respect of the power with which they are able to endow government, and the virtue of 'popular' institutions is recognized to be their capacity to provide government with greater quantities of power than any others. 'Democracy' is superior to 'monarchy' because it generates more power; 'divine right' cannot compete with a plebiscite as a source of power; and every extension of the franchise is seen to be an addition to the power at the disposal of government. If, on the other hand, the manner is that of scepticism, then the 'institutions' we are considering are understood principally in respect of their ability to control government, and the virtue of 'popular' institutions is their supposed preeminent capacity to do this efficiently and economically. 'Democracy' is superior to 'monarchy' because it more effectively protects the community against the pursuit of favourite projects by government; a plebiscite cannot compete with a House of Commons as a means of exercising continuous control over government; and every extension of the franchise is recognized as giving a broader base and more authority to this control.

But, we have seen, the manner in which a government is active in the modern world is rarely, if ever, a question of 'either–or'. There is a continuous scale, determined by the degrees of responsiveness a regime shows to each of the poles between which all modern regimes move.[6] Consequently, merely to defend or to attack 'democracy' is a meaningless activity – the relic of a remote epoch when governments were distinguished only in respect of their authorization because (on account of a general absence of power) there was, in practice, no opportunity for difference in the manner in which they were active. And the question, which has made itself heard since the middle of the last century, whether 'democratic' institutions can be made to 'work' is an ill-considered question: what is really being considered is whether 'popular' institutions can be prevented, in contemporary circumstances, from selling themselves entirely to the politics of faith. Nobody doubts that they are capable of preventing government from imposing a single pattern of activity upon a community. And when the question is reformulated in this manner, we perceive that we are no longer doing what we thought we were doing, namely, conducting an enquiry into the intrinsic qualities of 'popular' institutions: they have no intrinsic qualities but are amenable to either of the current styles of governing. What we are really considering is what chances there are of the sceptical style of politics recovering its vitality and restoring to our institutions and manner of government their obscured complexity and lost mobility.

Confucius, when he was asked what he would do first were he appointed governor, replied: 'the one thing necessary is the rectification of names.'[7] He meant that 'things' could never be 'straightened out' while words remained equivocal.[8] The observation was, of course, immediately appropriate to the politics of his situation, where government was not distracted between two opposed directions of activity. For us, for whom ambiguity of language is the reflection of ambivalence of activity, it is less appropriate. It is our predicament to be able to enjoy a complex manner of government only at the cost of an equivocal political

[6] Russia is a conspicuous example of the Baconian version of the politics of faith, as little hindered as may be by any modifying consideration, and established (as was to be expected) in a relatively simple community. What distinguishes it from earlier adventures in this style is the immensely greater power at the disposal of government; and what distinguishes it from most of the other regimes in Europe which have moved decisively in the direction of faith is the degree in which it has freed itself from every vestige of the pull of scepticism. The opposite of current 'communism' is not 'capitalism' (which is not a manner of government at all), but 'scepticism'.

[7] *Analects*, XIII. p. iii.

[8] Ibid., XII. p. xvii.

vocabulary. Nevertheless, the remark is not without its relevance to ourselves. And the virtue of the manner of political reasoning I have been investigating, if it has any virtue, is that it accepts what is undeniable and makes the best of it. By directing our attention to its ground and proper character it makes the ambiguity of our language a servant and no longer a master. And on the way it provides a means of removing some of the lesser confusions from our way of talking about politics: the subsidiary conflicts are seen to be subsidiary, and the counterfeit discrepancies are seen to be counterfeit.

INDEX

CPSIA information can be obtained
at www.ICGtesting.com
Printed in the USA
LVHW01s2358040318
568656LV00001B/133/P